Date Due

ALL ABOUT

Satellites and Space Ships

Sputnik

Earth

by **David Dietz**

**Sixteen-Page Photo Section
with Drawings by
George Wilde**

RANDOM HOUSE

NEW YORK

**allabout
books**

DEDICATED TO

Jimmy

Robbie and

Jackie

THREE HEIRS OF
THE SPACE AGE

CONTENTS

1. Dawn of the Space Age   1

2. The Ocean of Air   6

3. The Viking Rocket   14

4. From Fireworks to Satellites   23

5. Project Orbiter   31

6. Project Vanguard   41

7. Scientific Satellites   52

8. The Russian Sputniks   75

9. The Moon Messenger   83

10. Space Medicine   90

11. Passenger-Carrying Rockets   98

12. The Space Station   106

13. The Lunar Space Ship   115

14. Exploring the Moon   124

15. The Atomic Space Ship   132

16. The Riddle of Mars   140

17. The Solar System   148

18. Into the Milky Way   154

Index   161

1 Dawn of the Space Age

A new and exciting era in the history of the world has begun. It promises to be more amazing than any period in the past. It is the Age of Space Travel.

Over the centuries, courageous pioneers have crossed the oceans, the deserts and the mountain ranges of the world. Daring adventurers have reached the North and South Poles, climbed Mt. Everest and explored the dense jungles of Africa. They have ascended into the stratosphere in airplanes and balloons and visited the depths of the ocean in diving spheres.

Now they are preparing for the supreme adventure in exploration. They are planning the conquest of outer space. Their thoughts are turning to the moon, to Venus and to Mars.

The moon will be the first goal because it is our

nearest neighbor in space. It is only 240,000 miles away. To reach any of the planets it will be necessary to travel millions of miles. But once the moon has been reached, the courageous explorers of space will be eager to take off for those distant, mysterious worlds.

Scientists are already pondering over plans for space ships that can travel the vast distances that separate our earth from cloud-covered Venus and the red planet, Mars. Some of these plans are for space ships propelled by present types of rocket fuels. But many scientists are beginning to design new and novel types of space ships that will make use of atomic energy.

It is hard to say when the first journey to the moon will be made. Scientists are certain that it will be before the year 2000. It may be by 1975. Some scientists think it may be by 1965.

The first step in the conquest of space was taken in the year 1949 when the U. S. Armed Forces reached an altitude of 250 miles with a two-stage rocket.

The combination consisted of a big V-2 rocket, 40 feet long and weighing 14 tons, with a slim rocket 16 feet long, known as the WAC Corporal, mounted on the nose of the V-2.

The two left the ground under the power of the V-2.

At a height of 20 miles, the WAC Corporal was automatically fired and separated from the big rocket.

Because of the initial velocity given to it by the V-2, the little rocket attained a speed of 5,000 miles per hour and rose to a height of 250 miles.

At this height, the WAC Corporal had left more than 99 per cent of the earth's atmosphere behind it. So, for all practical purposes, it had entered interplanetary space. At 250 miles, the atmosphere is so thin that the few molecules of air in a given volume are about the same as those remaining in what we normally consider a very good vacuum in a radio or television tube.

While the newspapers of the world printed the news of the WAC Corporal's flight to the edge of interplanetary space, the event did not cause any great excitement. It was still felt that the era of space travel was a long way off.

But all that was changed with the second step in the conquest of space. This time the whole world was truly excited. No event had occasioned so much interest since the explosion of the atomic bomb in the last days of World War II.

This second step was taken on October 4, 1957, when Soviet Russia launched the first artificial satellite or moon. This was a metal sphere about 23 inches in diameter and weighing 184 pounds.

It quickly became known everywhere in the world by its Russian name of "Sputnik." Never had a new word become so popular and familiar in so short a time.

A radio transmitter in the sputnik broadcast a shrill signal. Scientists everywhere, as well as amateur radio fans, listened to its *beep-beep*.

On November 3, 1957, the Russians achieved an even more spectacular and exciting triumph, launching Sputnik II. This contained a live dog as a passenger.

The U. S. Army launched the first made-in-America satellite on January 31, 1958. It was sent up from Cape Canaveral, Florida, with a modified, four-stage Jupiter-C rocket. The Department of Defense named it "The Explorer."

The third step in the conquest of space will be the firing of a rocket to the moon. This will be only slightly more difficult than launching a satellite and undoubtedly will be done very soon. Perhaps it will have been done by the time you read this book.

The fourth step will be to fire a rocket that will sweep in a great curve around the moon and return to earth. If such a rocket is equipped with a television camera and transmitter, we will be able to see the other side of the moon.

New difficulties will be encountered when plans are made to send people to the moon. It would not matter how hard an unmanned rocket crashed against the lunar surface. If it went around the moon, it would not be too serious if it did not return to earth.

But once a passenger-carrying rocket or space ship takes off for the moon, the whole situation has changed. We must get our passengers safely off the earth. We must keep them alive in space. We must land them safely on the moon and keep them alive on the lunar surface. Finally we must get them safely off the moon and back to the surface of the earth.

But in spite of all the difficulties that must be overcome, scientists are certain that the first space travelers will reach the moon in the near future.

2 The Ocean of Air

Right over your head, there are strange and frightening contrasts. In the upper reaches of the atmosphere and the empty space beyond, there is cold more intense than the Antarctic and heat more broiling than the Sahara Desert. There are powerful rays more deadly than the fall-out of an atomic bomb and a penetrating rain of meteors moving with a speed of 40 miles a second.

Scientists must learn more about these regions before they can become cosmic travelers. Only then will they be able to direct their space ships up beyond the flickering rays of the Aurora Borealis or Northern Lights into the blackness of empty space.

We live on the bottom of an ocean of air, for the earth's atmosphere is a great sea over our heads. A rocket trip to the moon will begin with a journey through this ocean and will end with a return trip through it. We must learn how to navigate this aerial sea before we can venture beyond it.

We must know more about its winds at high altitudes, the variations in its temperature and density at different levels, the changes in its electrical and chemical behavior.

We must also know more about the sun's ultraviolet rays, the cosmic rays and the constant rain of meteors. On the earth's surface we are protected from these by the dense lower portion of the atmosphere. We will no longer have this protection in a space ship.

More information about the upper atmosphere will be useful for many reasons besides space travel. It will help us make better weather forecasts. Perhaps the day will come when we can predict weather a year in advance.

Improvements in radio and television will come when we know more about the ways in which radio waves are reflected by the electrified layers of the upper atmosphere. Perhaps we will learn secrets from the Northern Lights that will give us new ways of lighting our cities and homes.

Exploration of the atmosphere began soon after the invention of the balloon in 1783. In 1804 a balloon flight of a little over four miles high was made to measure the temperature, air pressure and humidity. Airplanes were used to collect similar information early in the present century.

In 1935 Lieutenant Colonel Albert W. Stevens and Major O. A. Anderson ascended approximately 14 miles in a stratosphere balloon. In 1954 Captain Ivan Kincheloe reached almost 24 miles in an airplane, the Bell X-2.

Unmanned balloons carrying scientific instruments, the big Skyhook balloons, have attained altitudes of 28 miles.

Rockets have done far better, carrying scientific instruments to altitudes of more than 100 miles. And now even more information is being gathered by means of the artificial satellites or man-made moons.

Skyhook balloons, rockets and satellites are being used to gather information about eight important things. These are: the composition of the air at different heights, the temperature, the density, the electrical conditions, the effect of the earth's magnetic field, the powerful but invisible ultraviolet rays of the sun, the cosmic rays and the meteors.

Rockets are also being used to photograph the earth from great heights.

Scientists divide the atmosphere into five layers and give each a scientific name.

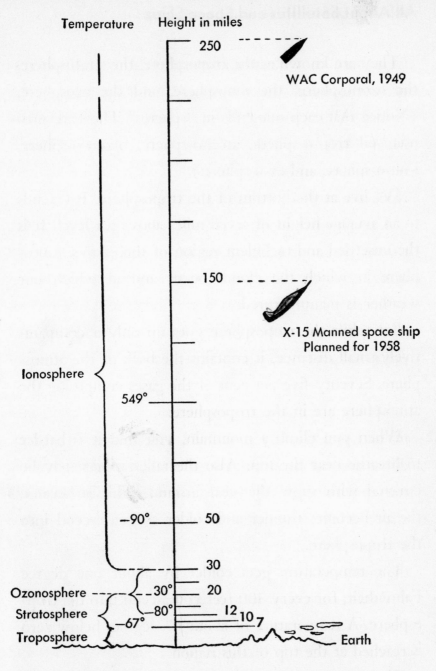

Temperature   Height in miles

250 --------- WAC Corporal, 1949

150 --------- X-15 Manned space ship
Planned for 1958

Ionosphere

549°

−90° ——— 50

30

Ozonosphere ----- −30° ——— 20

Stratosphere ——— −80° ——— 12 10 7

−67°

Troposphere ——— Earth

Above the ionosphere is the exosphere which fades into space.

They are known as the troposphere, the stratosphere, the ozonosphere, the ionosphere, and the exosphere. (Notice that each one ends in "sphere." They are pronounced trop-o-sphere, strat-o-sphere, o-zon-o-sphere, i-on-o-sphere, and ex-o-sphere.)

We live at the bottom of the troposphere. It extends to an average height of seven miles above sea level. It is the unsettled and turbulent region of the earth's atmosphere in which the clouds occur and in which our weather is manufactured.

But while the troposphere goes up only a comparatively small distance, it contains the bulk of the atmosphere. Seventy-five per cent of the gases composing the atmosphere are in the troposphere.

When you climb a mountain, you find it is harder to breathe near the top. Also the tallest peaks may be covered with snow the year around. This is because the air becomes thinner and colder as you ascend into the troposphere.

The temperature gets colder by about one degree Fahrenheit, for every 300 feet you ascend into the troposphere. A temperature of about 67 degrees below zero is reached at the top of this region.

The next layer is the stratosphere. It starts at the top

of the troposphere and goes up to a height of 20 miles. Powerful winds blow continuously in the stratosphere. There are two vast, swiftly flowing rivers of air, racing completely around the world, at the bottom of the stratosphere. These are the jet streams.

One of these rivers of air flows from west to east between the Arctic and the equator. The other flows from east to west between the Antarctic and the equator. Their exact positions and speed change from day to day. At times they reach a velocity of 500 miles an hour.

The existence of these jet streams was discovered during World War II when American pilots flew their B-29 bombing planes into the stratosphere.

In the stratosphere the temperature falls to 80 degrees below zero at a height of 12 miles.

The third layer of the atmosphere overlaps the stratosphere a little. It is the ozonosphere, extending from an altitude of 12 miles up to 30 miles. It is called the ozonosphere because it contains a form of oxygen known as ozone.

Strangely enough, the ozonosphere is warmer. The temperature here rises to 30 degrees above zero. This is because the ozone absorbs the ultraviolet rays of the sun.

The fourth layer of the atmosphere is the ionosphere. It is a strange and mysterious region of vacuum-like thinness where the Northern Lights flare and flicker. It begins 30 miles above the earth's surface. No one yet knows how far up it goes, perhaps as far as 500 miles. Scientists know something about the first 200 miles. The rest is hidden in mystery.

The ionosphere is a region in which no explorer could survive without protection from the powerful ultraviolet rays of the sun, the cosmic rays from outer space, and the deadly rain of meteors.

Life is possible upon the surface of the earth only because the bottom of our ocean of air is its densest part. Friction burns up most meteors before they can reach the ground. Only a small portion of the sun's ultraviolet rays and of the cosmic rays gets through the dense portion of the atmosphere.

The ionosphere contains a number of electrified or ionized layers of air. These form the "radio ceiling." Radio waves, leaving the antenna of a transmitting station, strike these layers and are reflected back to earth by them.

In the ionosphere the temperature drops once more, falling to 90 degrees below zero at a height of 50 miles.

Then, strangely enough, it begins to go up again, reaching the unbelievable temperature of 549 degrees at an altitude of 100 miles.

The fifth layer of the earth's atmosphere is the exosphere. This is the region where the atmosphere fades away into empty space. Very little is known about it.

Each day, billions of tiny meteors dash into the earth's atmosphere. Most of them are no larger than the head of a pin. A few thousand may be as large as pebbles.

When a meteor enters the earth's atmosphere, it is burned up by friction against the air. It leaves a fiery trail which we call a shooting star.

The Ocean of air

3 The Viking Rocket

The bright rays of the early morning sun shine slant-wise upon the sandy New Mexico desert. In dazzling flashes they are reflected from a slim pencil of aluminum that towers as high as a five-story building. The scene is the White Sands Proving Ground. A Viking rocket, carrying instruments for exploration of the upper atmosphere, is about to be fired.

The tall rocket rests upon a steel launching stand over the concrete firing pit. Its nose is pointed straight up. The scientists who will speed it into the sky have taken their positions at the control panels in the concrete blockhouse, 500 feet from the launching platform.

The blockhouse has concrete walls 12 feet thick and a floor of concrete equally thick. The pyramid-shaped roof, also of concrete, is 27 feet thick. The windows are narrow slits set with panes of glass 8 inches thick.

The construction of the blockhouse emphasizes the

dangers involved in firing a giant rocket. If all goes well, it will rise gracefully into the air. But rockets have been known to explode on the launching stand.

Preparations for firing the Viking began the night before when it was towed to the launching platform by a jeep. The rocket rode on a rubber-tired cart named the Barr cart after its inventor. Actually the cart consists of two separate parts. One, bolted to the nose of the rocket, has a single rubber-tired wheel. The other, bolted to the rocket's tail fins, has two wheels. All three wheels are equipped with airplane-type shock absorbers.

A huge gantry crane is used to put the rocket in place and to get it ready for firing. It consists of two rectangular towers of steel girders connected by a bridge of more girders at the top. It stands 60 feet high and is mounted on two pairs of rails 20 feet apart. There is one pair on each side of the launching platform so that the gantry can be brought directly over the platform.

The launching area is illuminated by a great battery of floodlights that turn night into day.

The hook from the hoist at the top of the gantry is lowered on its cable and attached to the forward wheel support on the rocket. The hoist is started and as the nose of the rocket rises into the air, the rocket rolls forward on its rear wheels. When the rocket is completely off the ground, the rear part of the Barr cart is removed.

The gantry now moves slowly over the launching platform, and the rocket is gently lowered until it is standing on its fins on the platform.

There are bridges jutting out at various levels from the two towers of the gantry. These enable the rocket crew to get at the little doors which open into different parts of the rocket. Often there will be a dozen men at work on these platforms, installing scientific instruments and making last-minute checks of gyros, electronic relays, valves and other parts of the rocket's mechanism.

If everything moves according to schedule, the rocket will be fired fourteen hours after it has been put in place on the launching platform. The time of firing is known as X and is counted backward.

The firing schedule begins, therefore, at X-minus-14-hours when the scientists mount the top bridge of the gantry and begin to put the scientific instruments for making measurements of the atmosphere, cosmic rays, etc., in the nose of the rocket. Each instrument is carefully checked to make certain that it will operate properly when the rocket is in the sky.

At X-minus-10-hours, the radio experts install the

radio transmitter which will send out signals by which the flight of the rocket will be checked. The transmitter is turned on for a trial check to make sure that the observing stations get its signal.

Tests of the rocket's radio cut-off mechanism are made at X-minus-5-hours. This is most important. The cut-off apparatus makes it possible for scientists in the blockhouse to cut off the fuel to the rocket's motor. They do this by sending out a radio signal if the flight of the rocket becomes erratic and the rocket gets off course.

Fueling starts at X-minus-3-hours. This requires the services of a trained and expert crew. First the alcohol tank is filled, then the hydrogen peroxide tank, finally, the liquid-oxygen tank.

Members of the fueling crew wear special protective clothing. Their heads are protected by hoods set with visors of clear plastic. Standing by the rocket, they look as though they had just landed from Mars.

Loading the liquid oxygen is the most spectacular of the three operations. There are two vents at the nose of the rocket which are connected to the oxygen tank. As the liquid oxygen, with a temperature of 300 degrees below zero Fahrenheit, is pumped into the tank, wisps of oxygen vapor appear at the vents, growing in intensity until they form heavy white plumes.

When the fueling operation is completed, the gantry is moved back on its rails, leaving the great Viking rocket standing alone on its launching platform, its nose pointed at the sky.

The launching area is now cleared of all fuel trucks and other vehicles, and the scientists and engineers take their stations in the blockhouse. The timekeeper stands at the microphone and announces, "Coming up on X-minus-15-minutes. Mark. X-minus-15-minutes." This means that if all goes well, the rocket will be fired in 15 minutes.

His voice is heard in the blockhouse. It blares forth from loud-speakers mounted outside the blockhouse as a warning to anyone still in the area.

Scattered over the desert and perched on surrounding mountains are a number of stations from which the rocket will be tracked by optical telescopes, radio and radar. The announcement of "X-minus-15-minutes" is flashed to all of them.

The scientist in charge is standing at the firing desk. At the back of the desk are two rows of meters. These tell what things are like in the rocket.

They are connected to the rocket by an electric cable. This cable runs to the top of a 40-foot pole about 20 feet from the launching platform. It loops over from the pole to the nose of the rocket. It will be disconnected automatically at the moment of firing.

Next comes the announcement, "Coming up on X-minus-10-minutes. Mark. X-minus-10-minutes."

Now the electric power is turned on in the rocket. When the switch is closed in the blockhouse, the electric impulse is carried over the cable to the rocket. It operates a relay that closes the electric circuits in the rocket. The gyros that control the flight of the rocket begin to hum.

The timekeeper now counts the minutes one at a time. At each count, one of the scientists pushes the switch that activates some control or instrument in the rocket. If his meters show that everything is in order, he pushes a button which causes a light on the firing desk to change from red to green. The scientist at the firing desk watches carefully to see that each red light changes to green as it should.

At the call of "X-minus-1-minute," one of the group pushes the switch which pressurizes the rocket's fuel tanks. He watches his meters carefully. If he sees that all is well, he gives the firing officer the green light.

There is now only one minute to the time of firing. The next call is "Forty-five seconds." The "All Clear" signal flashes on the firing desk panel.

"Thirty-five seconds."

The firing officer calls out, "Recorders on." The word is flashed to the radio receiving stations which will record the automatic radio signals from the rocket. At the command, they start their automatic tape recorders in operation.

"Twenty-five seconds."

At 20 seconds the timekeeper begins to count the seconds one by one, "Twenty, nineteen, eighteen, seventeen. . . ."

Finally, "Five . . . four . . . three . . . two . . . one . . . FIRE."

The firing officer has been watching the green lights. Had any trouble occurred, one of them would have switched to red. Now he pushes the firing button. An electric impulse travels over the cable to the rocket. Fuel flows into the rocket motor and is ignited.

The instrument cable drops from the nose of the rocket. There is a bright flash at the base of the rocket, followed by a mighty roar of sound as the fuel begins to burn. A shrill, piercing wail, like that of a siren, is added to the noise as the turbine and pumps reach full speed.

Now the rocket is rising from the launching platform. It seems to be balancing on the pillar of fire emerging from the nozzle of the rocket motor.

The rocket picks up speed, and the pillar is turned into a lashing fiery tail. Quickly the rocket gathers speed and is overhead, roaring out on its prescribed course.

Its flight is being watched carefully by the trackers with their powerful telescopes and by the radar people. The radio operators are watching their tape recorders on which signals from the rocket's automatic equipment are being received.

There is a charge of TNT in the nose of the Viking rocket, a small charge of only a few pounds. It is just enough to blow off the nose of the rocket when it reaches its maximum altitude.

This destroys the stability and streamlining of the rocket and causes it to go into a tumbling flight as it descends. As a result, it is slowed up and strikes the ground more gently than it would otherwise.

This gives the scientific instruments in the rocket a better chance of surviving the impact of striking the ground. It is particularly important if the rocket has carried cameras to photograph the earth or spectrographic equipment for recording the spectrum of the sun.

As soon as the rocket has landed, search parties, aided by the data supplied by the optical and radar tracking teams, start out to find it and recover the instruments.

4 From Fireworks to Satellites

The giant space ship that will take you to the moon one of these days will be the grandson of the high altitude rockets that are being used to explore the upper atmosphere and put satellites in the sky. These rockets are themselves the grandchildren of the spectacular fireworks skyrockets that go zooming into the sky at Fourth of July celebrations and burst into showers of fiery streaks and colored stars.

If you understand how these simple skyrockets work, you will have no difficulty in understanding rockets of any kind.

The simplest skyrocket consists of a little cardboard tube, five or six inches long, mounted on the top of a thin stick. The tube is filled with gunpowder and has a fuse at the bottom.

Rockets like this were made by the Chinese more

than 700 years ago. They used them to frighten and drive away enemies as well as for fireworks.

At an early date, the Chinese made improvements in the design of their rockets which are still found in fireworks rockets today. One of these was to put a cone on the top of the rocket so that it had a pointed end instead of a blunt one. This made the rocket fly better.

They also found that an extra charge of powder could be put in the pointed end and made to explode when the rocket landed among enemy troops. Today the cone of a fireworks rocket is loaded with colored stars.

The other improvement made by the Chinese was to scoop out a hole in the back of the powder charge. This made the powder burn faster, and so the rocket went faster. If a simple fireworks rocket were sliced open lengthwise, it would look like this:

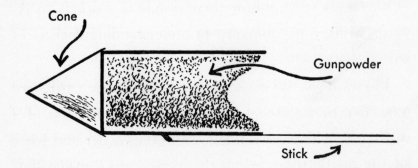

The secret of making rockets was learned by the Arabs from the Chinese and by the nations of Europe from the Arabs. Soon all the armies of Europe were using rockets. But by the year 1500 rockets had been given up in favor of cannon.

Improved rockets came back into use about 1800. The British used rockets against the United States in the War of 1812. You will recall that in "The Star-Spangled Banner" you sing of "the rockets' red glare."

Many people are puzzled about how a rocket flies and have quite confused notions about it. They imagine that the train of gases leaving the rocket pushes against the atmosphere. This is quite wrong.

The atmosphere is no help to the rocket. In fact, it is a hindrance since it offers resistance to the flight of the rocket through it. The rocket goes much more easily in empty space.

The behavior of a rocket is explained by a scientific law formulated by the great Sir Isaac Newton. It is known as Newton's third law of motion. It states that to every action there is an equal and contrary reaction.

If you have watched someone dive off a small float, you may have noticed that the raft dips into the water as the diver rises in the air. The downward movement of the raft is the reaction to the upward movement of the diver.

If you have fired a rifle, you will remember that the

gun kicks back against your shoulder. This kick is the recoil of the gun. It is the reaction of the gun to the forward motion of the bullet.

In the same fashion, the forward motion of the rocket is the reaction to the backward motion of the train of escaping gases, like this:

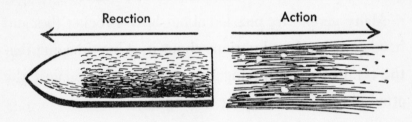

By about 1850 the armies of the world had given up rockets once more, and their principal use was again for fireworks. Rockets did not seem very important at the start of the twentieth century.

But all that was changed by a shy and retiring, but brilliant and hard-working, American scientist who gave his whole life to research on rockets. He was Dr. Robert Hutchins Goddard, Professor of Physics at Clark University in Worcester, Massachusetts. He is remembered as "the father of modern rocketry."

Dr. Goddard's experiments proved that the speed of a rocket depended upon the speed with which the train of burning gases was ejected from it. He soon realized that he could not build the kind of rocket he wanted with gunpowder as a fuel. So he turned his attention to liquid fuels.

On March 16, 1926, Goddard launched the first successful rocket using liquid fuel. This took place in the little town of Auburn, Massachusetts, on a snow-covered field of a farm owned by one of his relatives.

The rocket was a very light affair about 10 feet long. It used gasoline and liquid oxygen. A liquid-fuel rocket cannot draw its oxygen from the air as an automobile engine or airplane engine does. It must carry its own oxygen.

Goddard's little rocket stayed in the air for two and a half seconds and traveled a distance of 184 feet. That doesn't sound like much, but it was a beginning.

He continued to work on liquid-fuel rockets. Meanwhile other scientists and amateur enthusiasts entered the field; and rocket societies were formed in many countries, including the United States, England and Germany.

Before the reign of Hitler the German Army started a program which gradually grew bigger and bigger. Finally a huge establishment was built at Peenemünde on the Baltic Sea. Here the V-2 was developed. Major General Walter Dornberger was in command. Dr. Wernher von Braun headed the planning staff.

The first V-2 rocket fell on London on September 8, 1944. In the next seven months more than a thousand of them landed in or near London, killing about 2,000 people and doing much damage. No defense against the V-2 was developed during World War II.

The V-2 was a rocket 46 feet long and weighed 14 tons. It had a warhead which weighed one ton. Most of the rocket's weight was in its propellants. It carried four tons of ethyl alcohol and five tons of liquid oxygen.

Numerous smaller rockets were developed during World War II by both the United States and Britain as well as Germany. Many of these made use of improved solid fuels.

In these solid-fuel rockets, the fuel was carried inside the combustion chamber of the rocket motor.

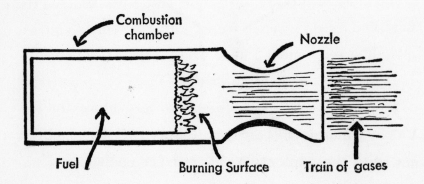

The simplest arrangement for a liquid-fuel rocket is to use a tank of some inert gas like helium or nitrogen to force the fuel into the rocket motor. Here is a diagram of such an arrangement:

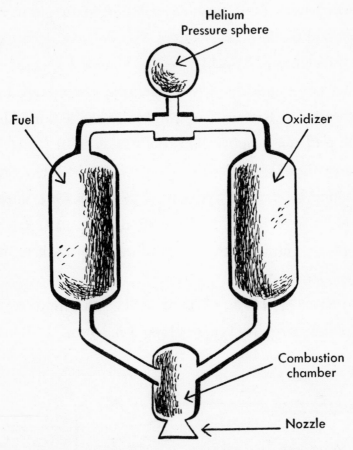

This arrangement, however, was too simple for the V-2 and the big rockets that followed it. The fuel did not reach the combustion chamber fast enough.

Pumps, operated by a turbine, were used to force the alcohol and liquid oxygen into the combustion chamber of the V-2. This turbine was operated by steam which was generated in a boiler by the reaction of highly concentrated hydrogen peroxide and potassium permanganate.

At the close of World War II, American troops captured a large number of V-2 rockets. These were used to start the high-altitude researches at the White Sands Proving Ground in New Mexico.

Later these studies were continued with two types of rockets developed by American scientists. One, known as the Aerobee, was a fairly small rocket, 20 feet long. The other, known as the Viking, was a big rocket about 45 feet long.

On May 24, 1954, a Viking rocket set a new record for a single-stage rocket, reaching a height of 158 miles.

5 Project Orbiter

Plans to add new members to the solar system were proposed by an American scientist at a conference in Oxford, England, in August, 1953. He was Dr. S. Fred Singer, rocket expert of the University of Maryland.

There had been earlier discussions of sending up rockets that would circle the earth and even plans for building a space station. But Dr. Singer's proposal was the first one for an unmanned satellite for scientific study of the top of the atmosphere and the space beyond.

He proposed a satellite about the size of a basketball. He called it the "Minimum Orbital Unmanned Satellite, Earth." This was a good name because the initials spelled "mouse." Thereafter, Dr. Singer's proposed moon was referred to as "the mouse."

His idea was to fill the interior of the mouse with scientific instruments like those which had previously been carried up in the noses of high-altitude rockets. Automatic radio transmitters would send the readings of these instruments back to the ground.

Such satellites would enable scientists to gather much more information than could be obtained with rockets. The flight of a rocket lasts only a few minutes. A satellite would remain in space for weeks, perhaps for months.

In the summer of 1954, a group of rocket experts met with high-ranking Army and Navy officers in Washington. It included Dr. Singer and Dr. Wernher von Braun.

Dr. von Braun assured the group that the Redstone rocket, which the Army had already successfully tested, could be used as the first stage of a rocket for the launching of a five-pound mouse. The Redstone rocket is a military rocket, patterned after the V-2. It was developed by Dr. von Braun and his colleagues at the Army Ballistic Missile Agency in Huntsville, Alabama. The Redstone has a five-ton warhead. Dr. von Braun's plan was to replace the warhead with a cluster of solid-fuel rockets.

The plan was given the name of Project Orbiter. It was proposed that the Army build the rocket and the Naval Research Laboratory furnish the mouse.

A few months later, a special committee of the International Geophysical Year asked the governments of the various nations taking part in it to consider launching satellites during the IGY.

The Army wanted to go ahead with Project Orbiter. The Navy wished to build a three-stage rocket using the Viking rocket as the first stage. The U.S. Department of Defense appointed a committee of nine scientists to study the proposals and it voted, 7 to 2, in favor of the Navy plan.

On July 29, 1955, the White House announced that the satellite project had been assigned to the Navy and that it would be known as Project Vanguard.

The schedule called for the launching of the first satellite in November, 1957. It was to be a small affair only six inches in diameter. The first full-sized Vanguard satellite was scheduled for March, 1958.

The Russians sent up their first sputnik on October 4, 1957. The American public was shocked and disappointed to learn that the Russians had succeeded in launching a satellite ahead of the United States.

There was a great deal of discussion of the American rocket program in Congress and in the newspapers. One result was that the Department of Defense told the Army to go ahead with Project Orbiter.

On December 6, 1957, an attempt was made to launch a Vanguard rocket at Cape Canaveral, Florida. It rose a few feet from the launching platform and then exploded.

A second attempt to send up a Vanguard rocket was planned during the week of January 19, 1958. Bad weather delayed the launching for several days. By that time, a fuel tank in the second stage of the rocket sprang a leak and had to be removed for repairs.

Meanwhile, Army experts had set up their rocket at Cape Canaveral. It was fired successfully on January 31, 1958, and put the first made-in-America satellite in the sky.

The rocket used by the Army was a special, four-stage version of the Jupiter-C rocket. It stood 68 feet and six inches high. It was designed by Dr. von Braun and his colleagues.

The first stage was a modified Redstone missile. This was a liquid-fuel rocket 56 feet long. For this occasion, it was equipped with longer fuel tanks than usual. It used a special fuel, known as Hydyne, and liquid oxygen.

The Redstone rocket was equipped with a detachable nose. The other stages and the satellite were mounted on top of this nose. These stages and the satellite ac-

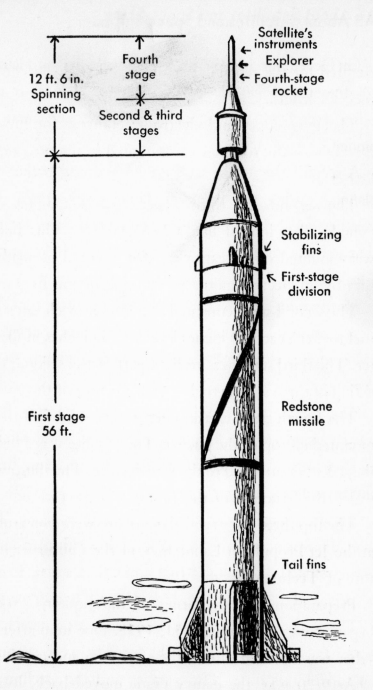

12 ft. 6 in.
Spinning
section

Fourth
stage

Second & third
stages

First stage
56 ft.

Satellite's
instruments

← Explorer

← Fourth-stage
rocket

Stabilizing
fins

First-stage
division

Redstone
missile

Tail fins

The Jupiter-C rocket was fired successfully in January, 1958.

counted for the remaining 12 feet and six inches of the rocket's length.

The gyroscopes and electronic controls for guiding the flight of the rocket were mounted in the nose of the first stage.

The second and third stages were contained in a cylinder that looked like a large bucket. This bucket was mounted on a bearing so that it could be made to spin by an electric motor in the nose of the first stage.

The second stage consisted of a cluster of eleven solid-fuel rockets, each 40 inches long and six inches in diameter. The third stage was really a part of the second, consisting of three similar rockets at the center of the cluster.

The fourth stage was another similar solid-fuel rocket mounted on top of the bucket. The satellite was a bullet-shaped affair attached to the fourth stage. The illustration makes the structure of the Jupiter-C rocket clear.

The top three stages and the satellite were constructed at the Jet Propulsion Laboratory of the California Institute of Technology.

Preparations for the firing of the Jupiter-C rocket began at noon on January 31, 1958. One item after another was checked during the afternoon and evening.

At 9:20 P.M. the gantry crane moved back, leaving

the Jupiter-C rocket standing alone on the launching platform. A battery of bright searchlights shone upon it.

At 10:25 P.M. the top stages of the rocket were made to spin. At 10:35 P.M. the radio transmitters were turned on. At 10:48 P.M. the scientist in charge pushed the firing button. This started a train of events that pressurized the rocket's tanks and ignited the motor.

Fifteen and three-quarters seconds after the button had been pushed, there was a bright flash at the base of the rocket and a great spurt of orange fire.

The gigantic rocket began to rise slowly until it seemed to be balancing on a pillar of golden fire. Then it gathered speed and zoomed overhead.

The first stage consumed its fuel in two and a half minutes, carrying the rocket to an altitude of 60 miles. At this point it separated from its nose and the other stages, and dropped into the ocean in a great arc.

The nose of the first stage, carrying the other stages and the satellite with it, continued to rise, coasting up to an altitude of 200 miles during the next four minutes.

During these four minutes, the electronic controls tilted the direction of flight until the assembly was traveling parallel to the surface of the earth. This was accomplished by the aid of a number of nozzles around the bottom of the nose. Blasts of compressed air were discharged through these nozzles from a tank in the nose.

During this time, its course was tracked at Cape Canaveral by four electronic devices. Two of them were radars. The other two were special radio devices which tuned in the radio signals from the assembly.

This information was fed into an electronic computer which told the observers on Cape Canaveral when the assembly had reached its highest point and was traveling parallel to the ground.

At that moment, Dr. Ernst Stuhlinger, one of the Army's rocket experts, pushed a button which sent a radio command to the assembly.

This ignited the eleven solid-fuel rockets of the second stage. The nose of the first stage dropped off, and the second stage burned for six seconds, increasing the speed of the assembly.

At the end of this time, the third stage began to fire and the empty shells of the second stage dropped away. The third stage fired for six seconds.

Then the fourth stage separated from the bucket and began to fire. It consumed its fuel in six seconds. By this time it was going over 18,000 miles an hour.

The empty shell of the fourth stage remained attached

to the satellite as the satellite went around the earth in its orbit.

The satellite was in its orbit six minutes and 48 seconds after the Jupiter-C had left the launching platform. The orbit made an angle of 34 degrees with the earth's equator. At its low point or perigee, the satellite was 219 miles above the surface of the earth. At its high point or apogee, it was 1,587 miles above the earth. It circled the earth once in 114 minutes.

The U.S. Department of Defense named the satellite "the Explorer." Because of the great height at which it circled the earth, some scientists thought that it might be a year or more before it encountered enough resistance at the lower end of its orbit to slow it up.

The Explorer is 40 inches long and six inches in diameter. This is the same size as the empty shell of the fourth stage which is permanently attached to it and going around in the orbit with it. The two together weigh 30.8 pounds.

The instrument package in the satellite was designed to measure the strength of cosmic rays, the intensity of the rain of meteors, and the changes in the temperature of the satellite.

The cosmic rays are detected by a Geiger counter. A

microphone in the satellite and gauges on its exterior detect the rain of meteors. Electric thermometers take the temperature of the satellite.

All this information is relayed to earth by two automatic radio transmitters, operating on frequencies of 108 and 108.03 megacycles.

The Army attempted to launch another satellite with a Jupiter-C rocket from Cape Canaveral on March 5, 1958. The rocket was fired at 1:28 P.M. and rose to a height of about 200 miles.

However, the fourth stage failed to ignite and the satellite did not attain sufficient speed to go into an orbit. It was burned up like a meteor as it re-entered the denser portion of the atmosphere. This ill-fated satellite was named Explorer II.

Explorer III was launched with a Jupiter-C rocket on March 26, 1958. It was launched at a bad angle so that the perigee or lowest point of its orbit was approximately 100 miles above the earth while the highest point or apogee was about 2,000 miles.

Because it dipped so low into the atmosphere at perigee, it was not expected to have a very long life.

6 Project Vanguard

Project Vanguard was started in the summer of 1955. On July 29th of that year, the White House announced that the Naval Research Laboratory had been instructed to design a rocket for launching at least six satellites.

Dr. John P. Hagen, a leading authority in the field of rockets, was placed in charge of the venture.

A three-stage rocket, known as the Vanguard rocket, was designed. Shaped like a rifle bullet, it is 72 feet long but only 45 inches in diameter at its base. It weighs eleven tons.

The first stage is a modified Viking rocket 44 feet long. It is a liquid-fuel rocket, using kerosene and liquid oxygen as propellants. These are forced into the combustion chamber by a pump operated by a steam turbine.

Steam is generated with the aid of hydrogen peroxide.

41

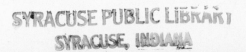

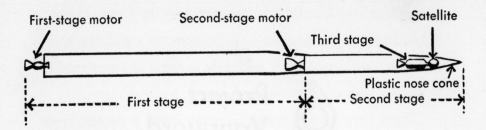

First-stage motor   Second-stage motor   Satellite

Third stage

Plastic nose cone

First stage   Second stage

A three-stage rocket, the Vanguard, was designed by the Navy.

There is also a sphere of helium gas which supplies the pressure to start the fuel system operating.

There are no fins or vanes to stabilize or steer the rocket. Instead, the motor of the first stage is mounted so that it can turn freely, changing the direction in which the jet of burning gases leaves the rocket. The motor is mounted in a gimbal like this:

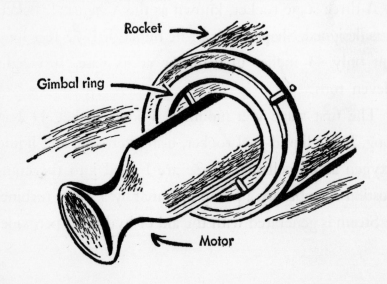

Rocket

Gimbal ring

Motor

The motor is hung on two bearings in a swivel ring. This, in turn, is hung on two bearings at right angles to the first two. Hydraulic controls govern the motions of both the swivel ring and the motor.

There are three possible deviations for a rocket from its course. These are known as pitch, yaw and roll. An up-and-down motion of the nose of the rocket is known as pitch. Left-to-right motion is yaw. Roll is a rolling motion around the long axis of the rocket. This is shown in the diagram:

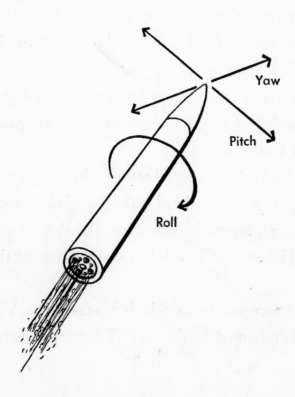

Yaw

Pitch

Roll

Pitch and yaw are controlled by moving the motor in its gimbal. Roll is controlled with the aid of the exhaust steam from the turbine that runs the fuel pump. The steam is ejected through a number of small jets around the bottom of the rocket.

The second stage of the Vanguard rocket is 28 feet long. It is also a liquid-fuel rocket with its motor mounted in a gimbal. The fuel is dimethyl hydrazine, and the oxidizer is nitric acid.

Because the second stage is smaller than the first, it does not require an elaborate pumping system. Helium under pressure is used to force the propellants into the combustion chamber of the motor.

To keep the second stage from rolling in flight, there are a number of tiny jets through which propane gas is expelled from a tank.

The third stage is a small solid-fuel rocket about three feet long. It is mounted inside the top of the second stage on a sort of turntable somewhat like that in a phonograph. The satellite is attached to the front of the third stage.

The electronic brain which controls the Vanguard rocket is mounted in the second stage just behind the third stage. The most important part of the control system is known as "the reference gyro."

The gyroscope is a wheel arranged in gimbals so that it is free to turn in any direction. A simple gyro mounted in gimbals looks like this:

Once the wheel has been set spinning in any given plane, it will remain in that plane irrespective of the motion of its supports. For this reason, the reference gyro in the Vanguard rocket immediately registers any deviation in the course of the rocket. The gyro detects where the rocket is in space and compares this with the desired course.

Acting through its various electronic controls, the gyro activates the mechanisms which control the motors and the auxiliary roll jets.

The success of the Vanguard rocket in putting a satellite into the sky depends upon the performance of a complex series of steps under the control of the rocket's electronic brain. We can picture the train of events which takes place when a Vanguard rocket is fired at Cape Canaveral.

The rocket stands upright upon its launching platform, a slim, gleaming, giant silvery pencil. Near by in the concrete blockhouse, scientists and engineers are making a last-minute check of the meters on the control panels.

As the time for firing the rocket draws near, a voice blares over the loud-speaker, "All stations, this is Project Vanguard coming up on X-minus-two-minutes. Minus two minutes. Mark."

The same announcement is flashed by cable to observing stations on islands in the Caribbean Sea and the South Atlantic Ocean. On Grand Bahama, San Salvador,

Mayaguana, Grand Turk, Puerto Rico and Antigua, scientists are waiting to track the Vanguard rocket with telescopes, radios and radars.

A minute later, the loud-speaker announces: "All stations, this is Vanguard Project coming up on 60 seconds. Sixty seconds. Mark."

Now the timekeeper calls out the seconds, one by one. He finishes, "Five . . . four . . . three . . . two . . . one . . . FIRE."

A flash of bright light, more intense than lightning, suddenly bursts forth from the base of the rocket. There is a mighty roar as the motor of the first stage begins to function. Slowly the great rocket rises into the air on its pillar of fire.

As the motor turns in its gimbal to stabilize the flight of the rocket, the fiery jet lashes about like a live snake.

The giant rocket rises straight up into the air. But 10 seconds later, the automatic controls shift the first-stage motor in its gimbal and the rocket begins to tilt into its prescribed course.

It is now traveling in a smooth curve to the southeast, settling into a path that makes an angle of 35 degrees with the earth's equator. But it is also climbing higher into the sky with every second.

Two and a half minutes after it has left Cape Canaveral, the rocket is 30 miles southeast of Florida and 36 miles above the Atlantic Ocean. Its velocity is about 4,000 miles an hour.

At this point, the first stage has used up all its fuel, reaching what the rocket experts call burn-out or *brennschluss*. (That word was borrowed from the German and means the same thing.)

The first stage is now only so much dead weight and so the rocket's electronic brain takes action. It sets off small explosive charges that shatter the bolts which hold

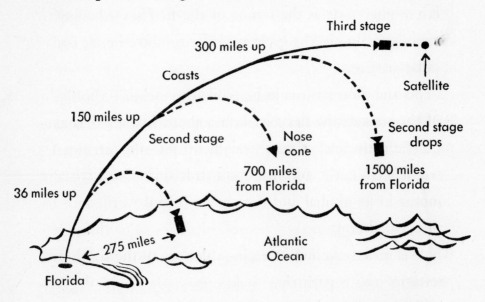

This shows the course of each stage of the Vanguard rocket.

the first and second stages together. At the same time, the electronic brain starts the motor of the second stage, and the second stage begins to pull away from the first.

The first stage continues to rise for a little while longer and then falls in a great arc, landing in the ocean about 275 miles from the Florida coast.

The second stage consumes its fuel in two and a half minutes, climbing to a height of 150 miles and reaching a velocity of 11,000 miles an hour.

Soon after the second stage begins firing, it has reached an altitude where the atmosphere is so thin that the protective nose cone is no longer needed. The automatic controls fire an explosive charge that splits it in two, and it drops off.

The second stage continues to coast upward after its fuel has been exhausted. Now the electronic brain has its most difficult job. Taking its cue from the reference gyro, it must get the second stage exactly on the desired course.

To do this, it makes use of auxiliary jets through which it ejects the helium which was used originally to pressurize the fuel tanks.

The second stage has now reached an altitude of 300

miles and is 700 miles from the coast of Florida, moving in an orbit parallel to the surface of the earth. Its velocity has declined to 9,000 miles an hour.

The time has now arrived for the final events in the launching of the satellite.

Tiny rockets, less than five inches long, are attached to the turntable that holds the third stage. These are now fired, and they start the third stage spinning. Since the satellite is attached to the third stage, it also spins.

The third stage now starts firing and leaves the second. At the same time, additional small rockets at the front of the second stage, known as "retro rockets" are fired. These act as brakes and slow up the second stage which falls into the ocean in a great arc, landing some 1,500 miles from the coast of Florida.

The third stage contains no guidance mechanism of any kind. The fact that it is spinning keeps it in its proper course just as the spin of a rifle bullet keeps the bullet on course.

In 30 seconds the third stage has speeded up to 18,000 miles an hour and exhausted its fuel. At this point, the explosive bolt holding the satellite in place is fired, freeing the satellite. A spring gives the satellite a kick, and it is now on its own.

The kick of the spring gives the satellite an additional boost in speed of about three feet per second.

The first Vanguard satellite, known as Vanguard I, was successfully launched on March 17, 1958. The Vanguard rocket which carried it aloft was fired at Cape Canaveral at 7:15 A.M.

Vanguard I is not a full-sized Vanguard satellite. It is only 6.4 inches in diameter. The launching was unusually successful, the satellite attaining an exceptionally high orbit.

At its lowest point or perigee it is 404 miles above the earth. At its highest point or apogee it is 2,466 miles up. Because of this, scientists expect Vanguard I to remain in orbit for decades, perhaps for as long as one or even two centuries.

7 Scientific Satellites

The gleaming artificial moons sent speeding around the earth may lead to new scientific wonders whose nature we cannot even imagine at this time. That is because the satellites are powerful scientific instruments designed to give us new information about the nature of the earth, its atmosphere, the sun, cosmic rays and the constant rain of meteors.

Satellites will also tell us things we need to know before we can build passenger-carrying rockets and manned space stations.

American scientists began designing the Vanguard satellites in 1955. They are marvels of scientific ingenuity. Each satellite has an electronic brain and a magnetic memory, as well as a radio voice.

The amazing thing about the scientific instruments

they carry is their small size. Some of them weigh only a few ounces. They are built with all the care and precision of a fine watch.

Each satellite is a hollow sphere 20 inches in diameter made of magnesium only three one-hundredths of an inch thick.

The exterior is gold-plated and covered with a coating of aluminum that gives it a bright mirror-like finish. There are four antennas for the radio transmitter, each about 24 inches long. They fold back when the satellite is in the rocket, but spring into position when the satellite is released.

With its instruments, the satellite weighs 21 1/2 pounds. Different types of instruments are carried in different satellites, depending upon what measurements are to be made.

The instruments are mounted in a metal cylinder that is securely fastened inside the satellite. At the bottom of the cylinder are the mercury batteries which furnish the electric power for the radio and other instruments.

Because of its small size, the radio has been named the "Minitrack." It weighs only 13 ounces. But despite its small size, it has a range of 4,000 miles.

An electronic brain with magnetic memory units is connected to the radio transmitter. This forms a "tele-metering system."

Information collected by the various scientific instruments is stored in the magnetic memory units. Then each record is played back in turn to the radio transmitter, causing variations in the *beep-beep* of the radio signal.

Receiving stations in the United States and elsewhere record the signals from the Minitrack radio on magnetic tape recorders.

The tape in turn is used to produce a visible pattern of jagged lines on movie film. From the pattern of these lines, the scientists read the information which the satellite collects.

The instruments in the various satellites had to be small. But also they had to be of such a nature that their readings could be converted into electrical impulses which the telemetering system could handle.

An ordinary thermometer could not be used in a satellite as it speeds around the earth, encountering the fierce heat of the sun in the daytime and the cold of outer space at night.

The thermometer used by the satellite is known as a *thermistor*. It is a tiny metal disk mounted on the outside of the satellite. An electric current is sent through it.

As the temperature goes up or down, the electrical resistance of the disk changes, and so the strength of the current changes. It is this change in the current which is stored in the magnetic memory unit and later broadcast to earth by the Minitrack radio.

Scientists are very eager to learn what the satellites will disclose about the rain of meteors. Billions of meteors enter the earth's atmosphere every day. Most of them range in size from dust particles to grains of sand. But some are larger.

Three devices spy on the meteors. One is an erosion gauge. This is a tiny ribbon of metal mounted on the outside of the satellite. The impact of the meteors wears it away.

An electric current passes through the ribbon and as the ribbon wears away, the strength of the current grows less and less. This decrease is recorded by the magnetic memory unit and later broadcast to scientists on the ground.

The second meteor detector is a microphone inside the shell of the satellite. It records the *ping* of meteors that strike against the satellite.

The third device is a pressure gauge inside the satellite.

If a meteor of sufficient size makes a hole in the shell of the satellite, this gauge will record the fact.

A meter set in the shell of the satellite records strength of the sun's ultraviolet rays.

One satellite has been especially designed to measure the strength of cosmic rays. It carries a cluster of Geiger counters for this purpose.

Another satellite will use an electric eye or photoelectric cell to scan the earth's surface. It will register the distribution of clouds. This information will help scientists solve many problems about the weather.

Elaborate plans have been made to track the Vanguard satellites from the ground with radio, radar and optical telescopes. Much important information will be gained from knowing the exact orbit of each satellite.

For this purpose, twelve radio stations have been established in a sort of picket line along the east coast of North America and the west coast of South America. These are known as the Minitrack receiving stations.

Each station has a set of eight antennas arranged in pairs. With their aid, it is possible to determine the exact position of the satellite. The stations radio their information to Washington where it is used to calculate the orbit of the satellite.

In 1949, the WAC Corporal rocket
reached a height of 250 miles.

Since 1946, giant plastic S
balloons have been used to
information about the atmos

A huge gantry crane begins lifting a Vanguard rocket into place at the launching pad.

The rocket stands on the launching platform as the hook of the gantry crane swings free. Bridges from the gantry structure enable the crew to get at the rocket for last-minute checking.

U.S. Army photo

This Aerobee rocket was launched in Canada to make weather observations at a 60-mile altitude.

U.S. Navy photo ▶

Less than a minute after take-off, the slender 23-foot rocket, Aerobee Hi, reached a maximum speed of 4,435 miles per hour.

The Jupiter-C rocket is prepared for delivery to the launching pad.

The satellite Explorer I and its booster rocket are checked before being mounted on the Jupiter-C rocket.

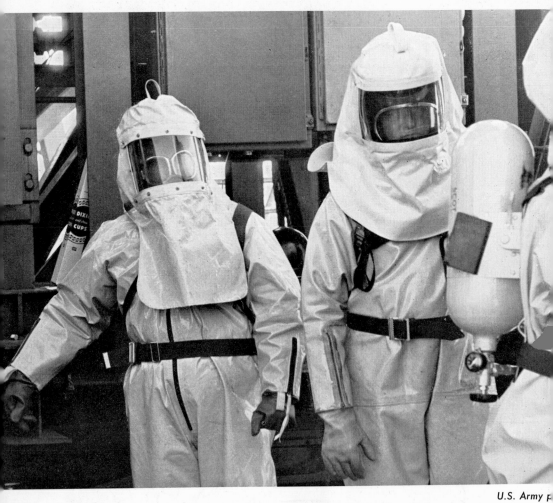

Service men in protective clothing begin fueling the giant Jupiter-C rocket.

The high-speed assembly of the Jupiter-C satellite vehicle is hoisted to the top of the main stage booster in preparation for launching.

The Jupiter-C rocket is shown on the launching pad.

The Jupiter-C rocket was launched January 31, 1958. Six minutes and 48 seconds after take-off, the first U.S. satellite was in orbit.

This miniature magnetic tape recorder was used to record and transmit scientific information from the Army's Explorer III satellite.

The giant 50-foot Diana radar "dish" at Fort Monmouth, New Jersey, was used to track the Army's Explorer satellite.

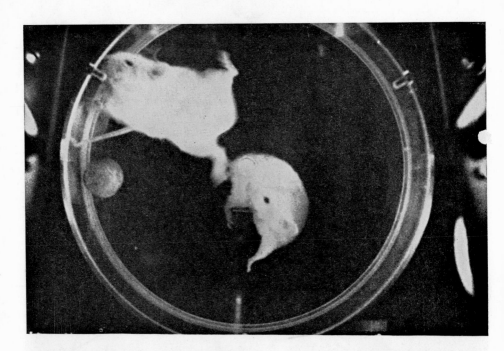

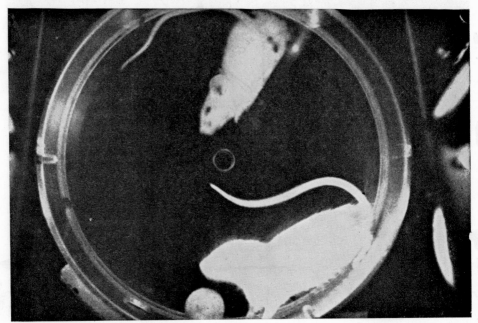

Pictures taken of mice in an Aerobee rocket show what happens without the pull of gravity. When floating weightless (top photo), mice are confused. When touching the surface of the drum (bottom photo), mice are perfectly oriented.

In February, 1958, Airman First Class Donald G. Farrell began a week-long make-believe "flight" in this experimental space cabin designed to imitate actual space travel. Airman Farrell suffered no ill effects.

At the Naval Research Laboratory, a satellite is tested carefully for resistance to shock, pressure, and vibration.

A recent photo of the moon shows the famous craters. When the picture is
turned upside down, the craters appear to be elevations.

This is a model of the Meteor Junior rocket designed to carry passengers into outer space. It is to be built by 1962.

More exact determinations of the orbit are then made with the aid of powerful telescopes which have been built especially for this purpose.

Amateur astronomers have been organized into teams in all parts of the United States to track the satellites with small telescopes. This program has been named Operation Moonwatch.

Among the powerful radar equipment which is being used to track the satellites is the big radar built by Massachusetts Institute of Technology on Millstone Hill near Boston. This has a great steel bowl 84 feet in diameter mounted on top of a 90-foot tower.

The exact determination of the orbits of these satellites will enable scientists to make better maps of the world and to calculate the exact shape of the earth.

We know that the earth is flattened at the poles and that it bulges at the equator. This is the result of the earth's rotation on its axis. But we do not know the exact amount of the bulge.

Maps of land areas, carefully made with surveying methods, are excellent. But these methods cannot be applied to the oceans, and it is believed that the location of many islands as shown on maps may be wrong by as much as a mile.

Such an error in a map can be serious for an airplane pilot who is making a long flight over the ocean and heading for a small island.

However, once the orbit of a satellite is known exactly, it can be used to calculate the exact position of a radio station tuned in on it. In this way the location of special radio stations which the United States is setting up on various islands in the Pacific Ocean will be determined. These include stations on Kwajalein, Luzon, Wake, Guam and American Samoa.

It will also be possible to calculate the exact position of the center of the earth with reference to the orbit of a satellite.

Once this is known, scientists can then calculate how far each station is from the center of the earth. From this information, the exact shape of the earth can be calculated.

⑧ The Russian Sputniks

Perhaps you saw one of the Russian sputniks go across the sky shortly after sunset or just before sunrise in the autumn of 1957. Looking like a very bright star, it traveled across the heavens from horizon to horizon in about five minutes.

You may also have heard the *beep-beep* of its radio, if you owned a short-wave radio that could be tuned to the proper wave length.

Thousands upon thousands of people in all parts of the world saw or heard the first two Russian satellites. Everyone called them by their Russian name of "Sputnik," and they became known as Sputnik I and Sputnik II.

Sputnik I was launched in secret by Soviet Russia on October 4, 1957. Its first *beep* was picked up by radio in the United States at 8:07 that evening.

It had been agreed by the member nations of the International Geophysical Year that satellites would have their radios use a frequency of 108 megacycles. It was found, however, that Sputnik I was broadcasting on frequencies of 20 and 40 megacycles.

As soon as it was known that Sputnik I was in the sky, the Smithsonian Astrophysical Observatory in Washington began to notify the Moonwatch Observers in all parts of the world by telephone, telegraph and cable. Working all night, the Smithsonian scientists got in touch with more than a hundred teams around the world before morning.

The twelve Minitrack radio stations which American scientists had established for tracking the Vanguard satellites were hurriedly converted from 108 megacycles to the frequencies being used by the sputnik.

Sputnik I moved in an orbit that made an angle of 65 degrees with the earth's equator. The orbit was not a perfect circle but a flattened circle known as an ellipse.

If a satellite were launched exactly parallel to the earth's surface and at exactly the right speed, its orbit would be a circle. Any deviation in direction or speed will result in an elliptical orbit.

Instead of having a center as a circle does, an ellipse

has two points known as the foci. The orbits of the earth and other planets are all ellipses with the sun at one focus.

It was found that Sputnik I was 150 miles from the earth at the lowest point in its orbit. This point is known as the perigee. At its highest point from the earth, it was 550 miles away. This point is known as the apogee.

The terms perigee and apogee have long been used to describe the points at which the moon is nearest to the earth and farthest from it.

The Russian newspaper *Pravda* disclosed that Sputnik I had been launched by a three-stage rocket. The satellite was 23 inches in diameter, and weighed 184 pounds. American scientists were surprised by the great weight of the satellite. It meant that a very large and powerful three-stage rocket had been used to launch it.

It was soon found that the third stage of the launching rocket and the nose cone which had protected the sputnik during the launching were going around the earth with the sputnik.

Moving with a speed of 18,000 miles an hour, the sputnik made one circuit around the earth every 96 minutes. Because the earth is turning on its own axis, the sputnik passed over another area of the earth's surface

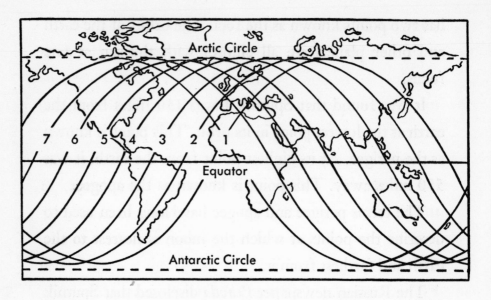

Due to the earth's turn, the sputnik took a new course each time.

each time it went around its orbit. The successive tracks
of the sputnik are shown on the above map.

At a height of 150 miles, there is still enough air to
cause some resistance to the motion of a satellite. As a
result, the orbit of the sputnik began to change, and it
began to spiral down slowly toward the earth's surface.
The same thing happened to the nose cone and to the
third stage of the launching rocket.

Finally, they descended lower and lower until they
got into air so dense that the friction caused them to burn
up like meteors. It is thought that a remnant of the third

stage fell to earth shortly after December 1, 1957.

Sputnik II was launched on November 3, 1957. It weighed 1,120 pounds, more than half a ton. This sputnik was not a spherical satellite but was actually the third stage of the launching rocket.

Inside this third stage were the radio and the various instruments for measuring temperatures, the density of the air, the sun's ultraviolet light and cosmic rays.

The biggest surprise of all was that it also contained a live dog as a passenger. The dog was a small-boned Eskimo dog of a type known as a laika.

The dog was in a sealed compartment which contained air-conditioning equipment and a stock of food. Instruments had been arranged to record the dog's breathing, pulse rate and blood pressure. This equipment was connected to the sputnik's radio so that information about the condition of the dog was broadcast to receiving stations on the ground.

Many people, both in the United States and Europe, were upset by the idea of this dog circling the earth in the cold of outer space, doomed to eventual death. But a larger number realized that the information needed for man to journey into outer space could only be collected by experiments such as this one.

Eventually, after some weeks, the dog died, a martyr to human progress like those dogs which had aided the progress of medical research over the years.

The orbit of Sputnik II was an ellipse. Its lowest point or perigee was only 100 miles above the earth's surface. Its highest point or apogee was 1,050 miles up. It took 103.7 minutes to make one trip around the earth.

The questions asked by many people after the Russian sputniks were launched showed that they did not have a clear idea of the behavior of satellites. The question asked most often was: What keeps the sputniks going?

The answer is that the sputniks kept going because there was nothing to stop them.

There was also a mistaken notion that the sputniks were outside the earth's gravitational field. Nothing could be farther from the truth.

It was the earth's force of gravity that kept the sputniks in their orbits just as it is the earth's force of gravity which keeps the real moon in its orbit. To understand this, we must have a look at Newton's three laws of motion. You will remember that Newton's third law of motion explained what made a rocket go. This law stated that every action has an equal and contrary reaction.

Now we need the first two laws of motion. Newton's first law states that every body continues in its state of rest or uniform motion in a straight line unless acted on by some force.

In other words, a body once set in motion, will keep going forever, unless it encounters some force which opposes its motion.

Newton's second law states that any change in speed or direction of a moving body is directly proportional to the force acting on it and the length of time that the force acts.

This explains why the pull of the earth's force of gravity keeps both the sputniks and the real moon in their orbits. If there were no force of gravity, the sputnik would fly straight off into space.

If the sputnik had no motion of its own, the earth's force of gravity would pull it straight down.

It is the combination of the two that keeps the sputnik in its orbit. At the same time that the sputnik is moving forward, it is falling toward the earth. At 18,000 miles an hour, the speed of the sputnik and the pull of gravity balance each other.

The combination is just enough to keep the sputnik

going around the earth, as shown in the following chart:

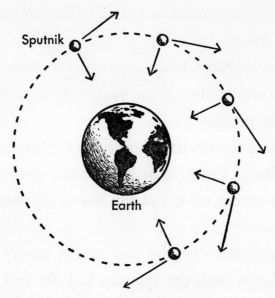

It is perfectly true, therefore, to say that a satellite is continually falling toward the earth.

The same thing is true of the real moon. It has been falling toward the earth for several billions of years. But it doesn't get there.

The sputniks would have kept going forever also if they had been higher in the sky. They lost energy because the lower ends of their orbits were low enough to encounter air resistance. As a result they settled still lower in the sky until finally they were burned up by friction against the denser part of the atmosphere.

9 The Moon Messenger

Now that satellites have been sent up to circle the earth, the next goal is the moon. An international race is on to see which nation gets the first unmanned rocket to the moon. Perhaps the race will have been won by the time you read this book.

Larger rockets than those which launched the satellites will be needed to reach the moon. But they are rockets which we know how to build today. They would not be very different from the intercontinental ballistic missiles which the military establishments of both the United States and Russia are now building.

Scientists have been dreaming of sending a rocket to the moon for a long time. The possibility was first pointed out in the year 1919 by Professor Robert H. Goddard, the great American rocket pioneer.

Goddard proposed loading such a rocket with magnesium powder, which would explode with a bright white light when the rocket struck the moon. He thought astronomers would be able to see the flash with their big telescopes.

There was much discussion of this idea in the years before World War II, and rocket enthusiasts coined a name for the first rocket that would reach the moon. They called it the "Moon Messenger."

Today it has been suggested that the Moon Messenger carry a hydrogen bomb. This would make a much bigger flash when it struck the moon, and there certainly would be no trouble about seeing it with big telescopes. Some people, however, do not like the idea of exploding an H-bomb on the moon.

Many scientists are convinced that much more might be learned about the moon by sending up rockets carrying scientific instruments to make a trip around the moon rather than smashing into it. Among the scientists in the United States who have studied this problem are Dr. George Gamow and Dr. Krafft A. Ehricke.

Dr. Gamow, who has a lively sense of humor, has proposed that instead of calling such a rocket a moon messenger, it be named the "Cow," in honor of the famous cow that jumped over the moon.

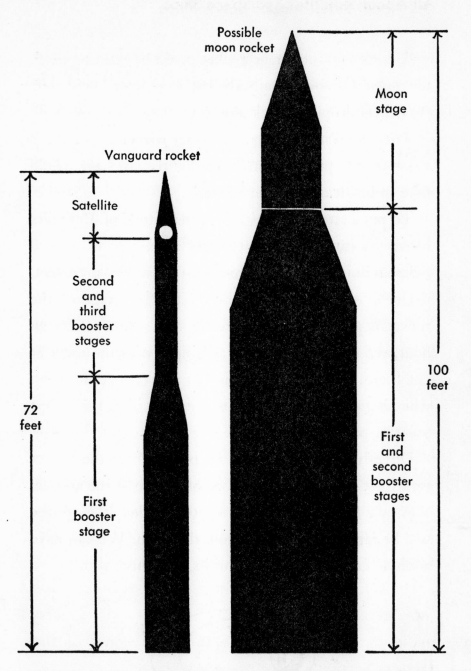

Possible
moon rocket

Moon
stage

Vanguard rocket

Satellite

Second
and
third
booster
stages

72
feet

First
booster
stage

100
feet

First
and
second
booster
stages

A rocket to the moon would have to be bigger than Vanguard.

All About Satellites and Space Ships

A three- or four-stage rocket could be used to reach the moon. Of course, only the last stage would get there, the others dropping back along the way.

The reason it would take a bigger rocket to reach the moon than to put up a satellite is that the last stage would have to be given a greater velocity.

To put a satellite into space at an altitude of 300 miles above the earth's surface requires a velocity of 18,000 miles an hour. If the launching of the satellite is perfect, the orbit will be a circle. But if the last stage of the rocket is given a velocity greater than 18,000 miles an hour, the orbit will become an ellipse with the earth at one focus. If the third stage is 300 miles above the earth when it goes into its orbit, this altitude will be the lowest point or perigee of the orbit.

Directly opposite will be the point where the rocket is farthest from the earth. This, of course, is the apogee.

As we increase the speed of our rocket, the apogee will be farther and farther from the earth. We can have a whole family of elliptical orbits, like this:

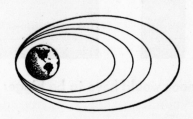

Of course, if we keep on increasing the speed of our rocket, we finally reach a point where the orbit is no longer an ellipse at all. At 25,000 miles an hour, our rocket reaches the velocity of escape and disappears into the solar system.

The moon's average distance from the earth is approximately 240,000 miles.

To send our rocket around the moon, we will have to give it a velocity less than the velocity of escape. If the rocket starts with a velocity of 23,900 miles per hour, the farthest point or apogee of its orbit will be 280,000 miles from the earth. If we time our launching properly, the rocket will go around the moon and return to the earth.

Perhaps you will be surprised to know that the rocket will not move with constant velocity. As the rocket speeds toward the moon, it will be rising against the gravitational pull of the earth. This will cause the rocket to slow up. The farther it gets from the earth, the slower it will move. It will be moving only a few hundred miles per hour as it goes around the moon.

Then, as the rocket returns to earth, it will gain speed because the earth's gravitational pull is now drawing the rocket back home. When it reaches perigee, it will again be moving at a velocity of 23,900 miles an hour.

It will take the moon messenger 157 hours or about six and a half days for the complete journey, and it will spend about 50 hours of this time rounding the moon.

As the moon messenger goes around the moon, its orbit will be distorted or bent by the gravitational pull of the moon. Scientists will have to allow for this when they determine the right moment for launching the rocket. If the messenger goes too close to the moon, its orbit will be bent so much that it will fail to return to earth and will go flying off into space instead.

The fact that the messenger will spend about 50 hours in the neighborhood of the moon, makes scientists very happy. If the messenger is equipped with a television camera and broadcasting apparatus, it will give us a better view of the moon than we have ever had.

In addition, and this is most important, it will give us our first view of the other side of the moon. Because the moon always keeps the same face turned toward the earth, no one has ever seen the other side of the moon.

Eventually, scientists would like to have a moon messenger that will return to the surface of the earth. If the messenger is traveling parallel to the surface of the earth when it reaches its closest point to the earth on its return, it will merely take off on another trip.

The trick will be to have auxiliary jets on the messenger slow it up and bring it into the earth's atmosphere. The danger will be that the messenger will now burn up like a meteor. But eventually a way will be found to bring a messenger back to the surface of the earth.

Such a messenger could carry motion-picture cameras as well as television equipment and would give us a permanent record of the moon's surface.

A scheme has even been suggested for bringing a sample of the moon back to earth. This would be done with the aid of a pair of moon messengers.

One would drop a small atomic bomb on the surface of the moon. The other would pass very close to the surface and would collect samples of the dust and rocks hurled into space by the explosion.

Such samples of the moon would help astronomers solve many problems about the nature of the moon and its origin. Of course, it would be necessary to have electronic controls of the most amazing accuracy to enable a pair of moon messengers to carry out this trick.

10 Space Medicine

A new branch of medicine has come into existence with the dawn of the Space Age. It is known as space medicine. The U. S. Air Force has a Department of Space Medicine.

The medical experts of these departments must solve many problems before explorers can visit the moon and the planets.

We must make certain that men can survive their journey into space, that they can take off safely from the surface of the earth, and that they can return in equal safety.

Some years ago the United States began to explore the problems of space medicine in two ways. One was by experiments with human volunteers in medical laboratories. The other was by sending animals on rocket flights.

American scientists sent up two mice and two monkeys in an Aerobee rocket from the White Sands Proving Ground in 1953. The animals were placed in an especially designed capsule.

The rocket reached a height of 36 miles at which the capsule was automatically separated from the rocket and returned to earth by parachute. On the take-off, the animals were subjected to a force fourteen times the force of gravity for two and a half seconds with no ill effects.

A motion picture was made of the mice during the flight. It showed they were very much confused during the portion of the flight where zero gravity set in and they became weightless.

The two monkeys were equipped with devices which recorded their heart beat, blood pressure and breathing. As soon as the monkeys were released from the capsule, one of them ate a banana with evident relish.

Russian scientists have sent up a number of dogs in rockets, some of them to a height of 60 miles. They reported that the dogs survived their journeys without ill effects. One dog, enclosed in a space suit, was ejected from a rocket at a height of 56 miles and returned to earth by parachute.

The dog in Sputnik II survived the upward journey

but eventually died in the satellite as it circled the earth.

A number of experiments have been conducted with human volunteers in an attempt to duplicate on earth the conditions which would be met in rockets or space ships.

Passengers in a rocket ship will be subjected to a strong force when the rocket takes off. The same thing happens on a modest scale in an automobile. If the driver starts too abruptly, the passengers are thrown backward.

The force thus experienced is measured in terms of how much stronger it is than the force of gravity. It is known as 2g, 3g, etc.

During World War II, it was found that airplane pilots, coming out of steep dives or sudden turns, could withstand a force of 4g safely. They blacked out at 6g. It was first thought that this would be the rule for rockets. But experiments have shown that the pilots blacked out because of their sitting position. As a result, the blood was drained from their brains; and this caused them to become unconscious.

Experiments have been conducted in the United States and elsewhere in which volunteers are whirled around a big circle on the end of a pivoted beam. The device is known as a centrifuge. The volunteer is subjected to a centrifugal force that becomes greater as the speed of whirling is increased.

At 3g, the volunteers complained of a great deal of discomfort and various unpleasant sensations including a distortion of the sense of time. But strangely enough, there was less complaining at 4g; and it was found that volunteers could take up to 10g. One exceptional man at Randolph Air Force Base could stand 17g.

The length of time during which these forces could be endured became less as the force became greater. Volunteers can take 7g for 10 minutes but can only stand 10g for two minutes.

Medical scientists are certain that passengers can withstand the force that will be encountered in the take-off of a rocket ship. Because the force is more easily withstood lying down, the seats will be tipped down so as to become beds at the take-off.

Lying on his back, the passenger will feel as though he were made of lead. At 3g, he will find it difficult to raise his arms or legs or head. At 8g, he will find it hard to breathe. But he will only endure this play of force while the rocket is accelerating.

When the rocket motors are shut off, the passenger will be faced with exactly the opposite condition—the sensation of weightlessness. Once the rocket is coasting under the momentum it has gained at the take-off, he will experience what is now called zero gravity.

Originally, this was known as "free fall" because it resembles the condition which is encountered in a fall from a high place.

Normally we are aware of our weight because the ground under us supports us and causes us to resist the pull of the earth's gravitational field. In a free fall, as for example a delayed parachute jump, the individual is falling freely with an acceleration due to the force of gravity. As a result, he experiences the sensation of weightlessness.

This same sensation will be experienced in the rocket once it is coasting, whether it is moving away from the earth's surface or toward it. The reason is that, in either case, the rocket is responding to the full effect of gravity.

The condition of weightlessness is a fact and not just a sensation. The passenger will find himself floating around in the interior of the rocket, walking as easily on the ceiling of the cabin as the floor.

If he lets go of an object, it will not fall to the floor of the cabin, but will remain suspended in space. It will be impossible to pour a liquid out of a bottle into a glass.

The big question is how the human system is going to react to this condition of weightlessness.

Weightlessness can be duplicated briefly with the aid of an airplane, and in this way the medical experts are finding out something about it. To date, the evidence has been somewhat confusing. Some pilots seem to find the sensation pleasant. Others just don't mind it. A minority find it decidedly uncomfortable.

The trick of achieving zero gravitation in a jet plane was devised by Fritz and Heinz Haber in the U.S. Air Force Department of Space Medicine at Randolph Field, Texas.

The pilot puts his plane into a steep dive, pulls out of it at top speed and cuts the power. The plane describes a parabola like the curve of a ball tossed by one child to another. During this time the pilot experiences weightlessness. Then he restores the power in his plane.

In this way, it has been possible to get periods of weightlessness of 30 to 45 seconds.

The first pilot who tried it reported that he felt as though he were sitting on a large globe which was spinning in several directions at the same time. He noticed that a pencil lying on the instrument panel rose up and floated in mid-air.

Twenty-two pilots enjoyed the experience at Randolph Field and reported a feeling of exhilaration and pleasantness. They did not have any sensation of motion but felt as though they were floating or drifting.

Eleven other pilots reported various sensations of falling, tumbling, rolling over, standing on their heads or being suspended in space. However, they were not particularly bothered by these sensations. Another fourteen pilots experienced all the symptoms of severe motion sickness and nausea.

From these tests, it would seem that some persons will find it possible to ride in rocket ships while others will not be able to take it.

Medical men and engineers are also studying the problems of designing cabins for space ships. Model cabins are being built at Randolph Field and elsewhere, and volunteers from the U.S. Air Force are trying them out to find out how livable they are.

Such cabins must be air-conditioned and pressurized. A supply of oxygen must be provided for breathing, and chemical means must be used to remove the carbon dioxide from the air as it accumulates.

Everyone agrees that controlling the temperature in the cabin of a space ship will be hard. During the take-off, when the rocket is rising through the lower part of the earth's atmosphere, friction against the air may cause the cabin to become extremely hot.

However, medical tests have shown that human beings can withstand temperatures of 158 degrees Fahrenheit for as long as 70 minutes without harm. Higher temperatures can be endured for shorter periods.

The sun's rays may cause the interior of the rocket to grow very hot. Some kind of shields or shutters will be needed to ward off too much sunlight.

Another problem not yet settled is the effect of cosmic rays. These are so powerful that they will go right through the skin of the space ship. More studies must be made with animals in rockets or satellites to determine how dangerous these rays will be to passengers.

11 Passenger-Carrying Rockets

Rocket experts believe that getting to the moon calls for a threefold program. The first part will be the creation of rockets that can carry men and supplies to altitudes of 500 to 1,000 miles.

With the help of such rockets, a space station will be built. This will be a gigantic version of the Vanguard satellites or the sputniks, in which men can live comfortably for months at a time. Building this station in space will be the second part of the program.

The third part will be the construction of the lunar space ship at the space station and its take-off for the moon.

You may wonder why it would not be simpler to build a space ship on the surface of the earth and take off directly for the moon. This certainly sounds a lot simpler, and perhaps someday it will be done.

However, it cannot be done today with the rocket motors and fuels now in existence. Calculations show that even if these fuels were improved quite a bit, a speed of 18,000 miles an hour is the best that could be reached with a single-stage rocket.

This would not be fast enough to reach the moon. It would only be fast enough to put the rocket in an orbit around the earth like a satellite. But scientists agree that it would be wasteful of fuel for this purpose. A three-stage rocket is more efficient because it drops the first and second stages after their fuel is consumed, thus getting rid of their dead weight.

Next, you may ask why it would not be possible to use a three-stage rocket that would take off from the earth. Such a rocket will probably be used to send an unmanned Moon Messenger to the moon.

Again, this would be a wasteful and inefficient way of doing it and would require too much fuel. Scientists are also agreed that the type of rocket needed for getting up through the dense, lower portion of the atmosphere will not make the best space ship. It will be possible, therefore, to build a much better space ship at a space station.

Even so, giant rockets of almost fantastic size will be

needed to carry men and supplies up into an orbit for the building of a space station. Present calculations show that it takes about half a ton of rocket on the ground to put a pound of material into an orbit around the earth.

Some years ago, Dr. Wernher von Braun proposed plans for a three-stage rocket as tall as a 24-story building. Such a rocket will weigh as much as a Navy light cruiser, about 7,000 tons. Most of this weight will be fuel.

On the take-off, the jet motors of the first stage will burn up 5,000 tons of fuel in a minute and a half.

Both the first and the second stages will separate after using up their fuel and will drop into the ocean. They will be slowed down by gigantic parachutes and by auxiliary jets which act as brakes.

The third stage will contain the cabin for the crew and passengers and will carry thirty-six tons of supplies for the construction of the space station.

The pilot will put this third stage into an orbit around the earth at an altitude of 1,000 miles. It will carry a reserve supply of fuel so that he can bring it back to earth again.

Von Braun pictured a third stage with wings like an

airplane so that it can glide to earth when it re-enters the atmosphere.

Plans for a passenger-carrying, three-stage rocket were also made by three experts of the Goodyear Aircraft Corporation, Darrell C. Romick, Richard E. Knight and J. M. van Pelt. They called their proposed rocket the "Meteor."

More recently, Romick, Knight and Samuel Black have designed a smaller version of the Meteor which they call "Meteor Junior." They believe that this can be built by 1962.

Each stage of Meteor Junior will have wings like an airplane and will carry a crew so that it can be brought back safely to earth.

The first stage will weigh 500 tons and will have a battery of 17 rocket motors. Some of these will be in gimbals. There will also be auxiliary jets at the wing tips and tail fins for controlling its course.

A pilot, a co-pilot and a flight engineer will be in the cabin of the first stage. After separation from the second stage, the first stage will return to earth. Special doors will close the nose of the first stage to preserve its stream-line form. When it enters the lower part of the atmosphere, the pilot will guide it into a gentle glide which will bring it down to earth.

The second stage will weigh 70 tons and will have six rocket motors. In most respects it will be a smaller copy of the first stage. It will carry a pilot and a co-pilot to bring it back to earth.

The third stage will weigh six tons and will have four rocket motors, all of them mounted in gimbals. It will have a cabin space for a crew of three and for four additional passengers. It will also have room for about half a ton of cargo.

The pilot of the third stage will be the command pilot of the rocket. He will direct the take-off and the separation of the first two stages.

The first stage will reach a speed of 6,000 miles an hour, the second stage, 15,000, and the third stage, 18,000. The command pilot will put the third stage into an orbit at an altitude of 500 miles. The flight engineer will then turn off the rocket motors, and the third stage will stay in this orbit as long as desired.

The third stage always points in the same direction. Consequently it is traveling nose first in half of its orbit and tail first in the other half. To return to earth, the command pilot will start the rocket motors when he is traveling tail first. They will now act as brakes and slow up the rocket.

As a result, the orbit will change from a circle to an ellipse, dipping down to within 64 miles of the earth's surface. At this altitude there will be enough air resistance to slow the rocket down still more, and it will gradually glide to earth under the control of the pilot.

Pilots will need a great deal of experience to handle a three-stage rocket like Meteor Junior. But that skill and knowledge is already being obtained with rocket planes. The armed forces of the United States have been experimenting with rocket planes for some years.

The first plane to fly faster than the speed of sound, the Bell X-1, was a rocket plane. In 1956, Captain Ivan Kincheloe took the Bell X-2 to an altitude of almost 24 miles, setting a record for airplane flight.

Sometime during 1959, Kincheloe is scheduled to make a flight in a new rocket plane, the X-15.

The little rocket plane will be suspended just below the belly of a big bomber, either a B-36 or a B-52. The bomber will carry it up to an altitude of 8 miles.

At this point, Kincheloe will climb down into the X-15. He will wear a pressurized space suit. He will strap himself into the cockpit and close the canopy overhead.

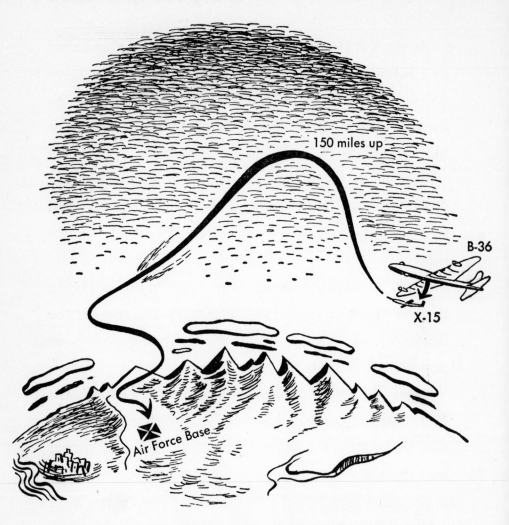

150 miles up

B-36

X-15

Air Force Base

This shows the probable route of the rocket plane X-15.

When he gives the signal, the big bomber will drop the X-15 and bank quickly out of the way. Kincheloe will start the rocket motor and pull back on the stick, pointing the plane up at an angle of 45 degrees.

As the X-15 gathers speed, Kincheloe will be subjected to a force of acceleration equal to about 4g. His body will feel as heavy as lead as the plane climbs up through the cold reaches of the stratosphere and into the vacuum-like thinness of the ionosphere.

The rocket plane will reach a maximum speed of 3,600 miles an hour or a mile a second. It is expected to climb higher than 100 miles, perhaps as high as 150 miles.

Then Kincheloe will start back to earth. He will bring the plane back in a long gradual glide so as to re-enter the denser lower portion of the atmosphere as slowly as possible.

Later on, other experiments may be tried with the X-15. One suggestion is to fit it with booster rockets so that it can gain still greater speed and climb still higher into the sky.

As pilots learn to bring such rocket planes as the X-15 safely back to earth, designers will be able to start work on rocket transports for carrying passengers and freight from one city to another. Many experts think that in the near future it will be possible to make a trip from New York to San Francisco or across the Atlantic Ocean in less than an hour.

12 The Space Station

The space station will be built in space, in an orbit high above the top of the atmosphere. Most experts would prefer an altitude of 1,000 miles, but it is probable that the first space station will be built at 500 miles. This will be easier to do and so can be done sooner.

Giant three-stage rockets like the Meteor Junior will bring men and supplies to an altitude of 500 miles.

Materials brought up by these transport rockets will be dumped into space. The engineers and technicians, wearing suitable space suits, will calmly step out of the rockets into space.

Do you have visions of men and material falling to earth, descending in great arcs and burning up like meteors in the dense lower regions of the atmosphere?

This will not happen. When the third stage of a

transport rocket reaches an altitude of 500 miles, the pilot will put it into an orbit like a satellite. Since there is no air at this altitude, the rocket will keep in its orbit as long as desired.

Now it is obvious that everything inside the rocket is moving with the speed of the rocket. So anything shoved out of the rocket will continue to move with this speed.

If a load of steel girders is dumped out of the rocket, it will continue to circle the earth in the same orbit with the rocket. The same thing will happen to the engineer who steps out of the rocket in a space suit.

An interesting fact is that the men who step out in space will not have any sensation of moving at great speed. The earth is going around the sun with a speed of 18½ miles a second, but you and I do not have any sensation of moving through space.

A number of plans have been put forward for the design of a space station. It has even been suggested that one could be built out of light plastic materials with walls of nylon. Since the space station is in empty space, it does not need any protection from the atmosphere. There is some question, however, as to what meteors might do to a station of such light construction.

One of the best known plans for a station is that put

forward by Dr. Wernher von Braun. His design looks like a big wheel.

The main portion of the station is the rim of the wheel. There is a small central structure at the hub of the wheel and corridors that run like spokes from the hub to the rim.

He has suggested that the wheel be made to rotate as it goes around its orbit. Centrifugal force would then take the place of gravity and the scientists and engineers in the station would not experience the sensation of weightlessness.

Such a station may be as much as 250 feet in diameter. It will contain machine shops and scientific laboratories as well as living quarters for scientists and engineers.

The space station will serve a triple purpose. It will be the "shipyard" where space ships are built. It will also serve as a terminal for these ships. Returning from the moon or Mars, the space ships will leave their passengers at the station. Transport rockets will then take them back to the surface of the earth.

The third purpose of the station will be scientific research. It will be equipped with telescopes and Geiger counters and other apparatus for studying the sun, the stars, cosmic rays and the other wonders of the universe.

Von Braun suggests a wheel-shaped space station like this.

Some of these instruments will also be turned on the earth below to study the clouds and the changes in the weather.

Many experts regard the plan for a space station suggested by Dr. Darrell C. Romick as the best put forward so far. Romick would use the third stage of the Meteor Junior rocket in the construction of his station.

Two of the third stages will be joined, nose to nose, to form the central core of the Meteor Junior space station. The wings and tail fins will then be removed and the rocket motors taken out of them.

This will result in a long, tubular structure which will form the core of the Meteor Junior space station. In fact, as soon as the core has been put together, it can be used as a space station, although it will be a small one.

Other transport rockets will bring up more structural parts and a larger station, tubular in form, will be built around the core. The illustrations make this clear.

Finally, living quarters will be built at one end of the station in the form of a gigantic wheel which will be made to rotate.

The reason for rotating the living quarters, of course, is to provide a centrifugal force which will eliminate the sensation of weightlessness.

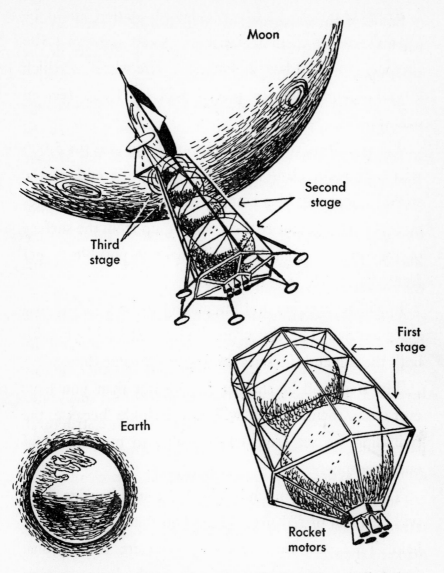

Moon

Second
stage

Third
stage

First
stage

Earth

Rocket
motors

As Meteor Junior nears the moon, the first stage will drop.

Romick points out that the space station could be expanded to any desired size. He suggests a station 1,500 feet long and 500 feet in diameter. The wheel in which the living quarters are placed will be 1,000 feet in diameter.

There will be room in a station of this size for 5,000 scientists, technicians and visitors. At one end of the station, there will be a landing dock for the third stages of the Meteor Junior rockets coming up from the surface of the earth. An air lock will make it possible to get from the rocket into the station.

It will be exciting and fascinating to be a visitor in a space station. The sky around you will be black with both the sun and the stars shining at the same time.

The stars will be sharper and clearer than you have ever seen them. They will not twinkle because the twinkling we see from earth is due to movements of our atmosphere.

The sun will be much brighter. Around its edge there will be a rim of red fire and beyond that a great silvery halo. These are the sun's chromosphere and corona, features that are only seen from earth during a total eclipse of the sun.

You will see the earth as a great globe surrounded by a blue haze. With the aid of binoculars or a small telescope, you will have no difficulty in making out rivers and mountains, coastlines and oceans.

You will have the sensation that the space ship is standing still and that the earth is going around you, just as now you feel as though the earth is standing still while the sun goes across the heavens from sunrise to sunset.

Building the space station will not be easy. It calls for the solution of many problems. The first is to design space suits which will enable engineers and technicians to step out into space.

These suits will have to be made of metal or plastic, and they will have to be pressurized. Each man will also have to carry an oxygen supply on his back.

Engineers and mechanics who assemble the space station will want ropes or cables to anchor them to their work. This is not because of any fear of falling, but to keep them from drifting away.

The largest steel girder will be weightless as it goes around the orbit. It will be no trick at all for a man to push such a girder around. But once it starts moving in a given direction, it will continue to drift away unless stopped. That is why anchor ropes will be needed to keep men and material together.

It is possible that small "space taxis" will be developed for getting around during the construction job. These will need very little rocket power.

Workmen will have to get used to working in space. On the surface of the earth, the sunlight is scattered in all directions by the molecules of air. But in space the sunlit side of an object will be intensely bright. The opposite side will be lost in blackness. Empty space will be black, not blue like the sky we see.

These peculiar lighting effects will make it difficult for the workmen who are putting the space station together.

The men will also be bothered by temperature effects. Objects will be subjected to the direct rays of the sun. An object in the sunlight will become extremely hot while one in shadow will be extremely cold.

13 The Lunar Space Ship

The first space ship that takes off for the moon will look quite different from the sleek, powerful rockets with which you are familiar. At first glance, it will appear flimsy and rickety. You will wonder how it could survive the journey to the moon.

The reason for this is that it will be built at the space station, 500 to 1,000 miles above the surface of the earth. It does not have to rise through the dense lower portion of the earth's atmosphere. Consequently, it does not need the streamlined design and the tough skin of a rocket that leaves the earth's surface.

The shape of the ship will have no particular influence on its progress through outer space. It will be possible, for example, to put several large, mirror-like radar antennas on the lunar space ship.

Most of the space ships that have been designed so far

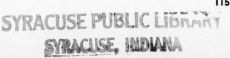

have the fuel tanks, rocket motors and other parts completely exposed and held together by a light frame of steel or aluminum.

Of course, an important part of a lunar space ship is a cabin for the crew and passengers. This must be designed carefully.

Getting to the moon will not take as much fuel as you might think, even though the moon is 240,000 miles away. Perhaps you picture the space ship leaving the space station and heading straight for the moon just as an airplane flies from New York to Chicago. It would not be done that way.

Since the lunar ship will be built at the space station, it will already be circling the earth with the velocity of the space station. This will be something less than 18,000 miles, depending upon the exact altitude of the station above the surface of the earth.

To get to the moon, the pilot will fire the ship's rocket motors just long enough to increase the speed of the ship to about 23,000 miles an hour.

This will put the ship into an elliptical orbit like that suggested for the Moon Messenger. The lowest point, or perigee, of this orbit will be at the altitude of the space station. The highest point, or apogee, will be a little beyond the moon.

Therefore, the lunar ship will start for the moon by swinging around the earth and going into an elliptical orbit.

It is entirely possible that on the first trip to the moon there will be no attempt to land on the moon. The lunar ship will merely go around the moon and return.

As the lunar ship approaches the moon, it will move more and more slowly. This is because the ship is constantly rising against the earth's force of gravity on its way to the moon.

As a result, it will take the lunar ship about 75 hours to get to the neighborhood of the moon. It will then have slowed down so much that, like the Moon Messenger, it will take about 50 hours to swing around the moon.

On the return journey, it will pick up speed since the earth's force of gravity is now pulling the ship toward the earth. By the time the ship has returned to the neighborhood of the space station, it will again be moving with the same velocity that it started up. The whole trip will take 157 hours.

When the lunar ship is in the neighborhood of the

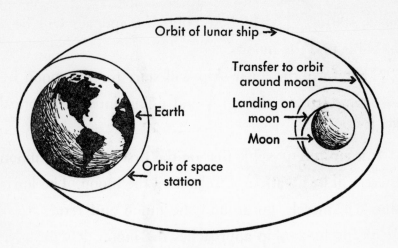

The lunar space ship can swing around the moon in about 50 hours.

moon, the pilot can change the orbit of the ship, if he wishes, so as to go in a circle around the moon. To do this, he will turn the space ship tail first and fire his motors for a brief time. The jets will now act as a brake and slow up the ship.

The ship will now become a satellite of the moon, going around the moon under the influence of the moon's force of gravity.

If the pilot has decided to land on the moon, he will circle the moon a number of times in order to pick out a suitable landing spot. He will then fire his motors again, slowing up the ship still more and coming down to the moon's surface in a spiral.

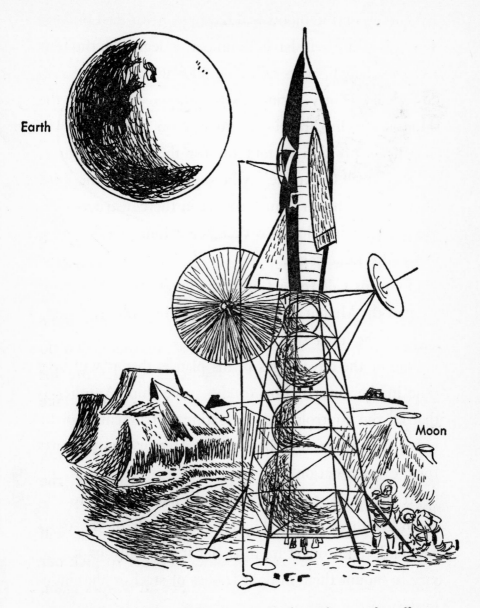

Meteor Junior will land on its tail ready to take off.

Landing on the moon will require a great deal of care. The space ship will have a number of legs, like those of a camera tripod, at its tail. The pilot will bring the ship down very gently, firing his motors to slow down the ship and finally bringing it to rest on its legs. It will then be in position to take off for the return journey.

Dr. Darrell C. Romick, who suggested using the third stage of the Meteor Junior rocket in the construction of the space station, has also designed a lunar ship making use of this same stage.

His plans call for a four-stage lunar ship. The third stage of the Meteor Junior rocket will become the fourth stage of the lunar ship.

One of the advantages of his plan is that it will save time in the construction of the space ship. Another is that all the controls and navigating instruments can be tested on the ground before the Meteor Junior starts for the space station.

At the space station, it will only be necessary to add the other three stages. These will be built of the usual fuel tanks and rocket motors. But it will only be necessary to mount them in light frames of steel or aluminum girders.

The first stage will be fired to put the lunar ship into

an elliptical orbit on the take-off from the space station. Once this stage has consumed its fuel, it will be separated from the lunar ship and abandoned in space.

When the ship is in the neighborhood of the moon, the motors of the second stage will be fired, first to put the ship into an orbit around the moon and then to bring it down to the lunar surface. The ship will land tail first and come down upon its legs, as you see in the illustration.

The fuel supply of the second stage will be exhausted in landing on the moon. Consequently, when it is time to leave the moon, the second stage will be disconnected, serving merely as a launching platform.

The motors of the third stage will now be started and the lunar ship will rise from the surface of the moon, leaving the second stage behind. It will be easier to put the ship back in its elliptical orbit than it was to get it into this orbit originally. This is because the gravitational pull of the moon is only one-sixth that of the earth.

When the lunar ship has returned to the neighborhood of the space station, the pilot can abandon the third stage. He can now discharge his passengers at the space station. Or he can use the motors of the fourth stage to slow it up and go into a small elliptical orbit that will bring it into the dense portion of the atmosphere. From here he will glide to a landing on the surface of the earth.

A trip to the moon will be an exciting experience. You will go by auto to the launching field just as you now go to the airport to catch a plane.

An elevator will take you up one of the towers of the gantry crane and you will cross the gangplank that takes you into the cabin of the third stage of the transport rocket.

When all the passengers are in, the doors of the cabin will be tightly closed and the air-conditioning apparatus will be turned on. Then the gantry crane will move out of the way.

The command pilot will check his instruments and then give the signal for the take-off.

At the take-off, your seat and those of the other passengers will be tipped back to form beds. There will be a tremendous, rumbling roar as the motors of the first stage ignite. As the rocket rises into the air, you will feel a pressure of about 4g.

But in a couple of minutes, the motors will have consumed their fuel and now you will feel weightless. Looking out of the portholes, you will see the earth far below and you will be able to recognize that it is a globe. As you rise, the sky will get less and less blue. Finally, it will be black and you will see the stars as well as the sun.

You will feel an increase in "g" when the motors of the second stage are fired and again when the third-stage motors are ignited.

Arriving at the space station, you will transfer from the cabin of your rocket to the station through an air lock. After dinner in the station, you will go through the air lock once more, this time to take your place in the cabin of the lunar ship. You will be on your way to the moon.

14 Exploring the Moon

The so-called Man in the Moon seems to smile at us as our lunar ship fires its motors and leaves the space station behind. The moon looks brighter and more silvery than we have ever seen it from earth, for now there is no atmosphere to interfere with our view.

As the hours go by, the moon grows in size and brightness. Soon we have such a view of the moon as we can get on earth with the aid of a good pair of prism binoculars or a small telescope.

Now we see that the Man in the Moon is really a series of large dark areas on the surface of the moon. We also see the great ranges of mountains that surround these areas and the wild profusion of large and small craters that dot the whole visible surface of the moon.

This was the way the moon looked to Galileo when he turned his first little telescope upon its silvery disk in the year 1609. He thought the dark areas were oceans and so he called them *maria,* the Latin word for "seas."

We know today that the moon has neither air nor water and that what Galileo thought were seas are only great flat plains.

However, we still call these areas by the poetic names that were given to them in the time of Galileo. These names were in Latin and so we speak of the *Mare Sereni-tatis* or Sea of Serenity, the *Mare Tranquilitatis* or Sea of Tranquility, the *Mare Imbrium* or Sea of Rains, and so on.

Astronomers have been making maps of the moon since the time of Galileo, and our navigator has some of the more recent lunar maps with him. These maps give us the names of mountain ranges and craters as well as the maria.

But even more important to us than the maps, are the photographs of the moon which he has with him. These were made with the giant telescopes at Mt. Wilson and Palomar Mountain. They show us the surface of the moon as we would see it if we were only 200 miles from the moon.

When we are only 200 miles from the moon, the pilot of our space ship puts it into a circular orbit around the

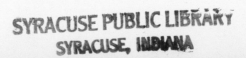

moon. Now we see it with our unaided eye just as astronomers have previously seen it with the great 100-inch telescope on Mt. Wilson and the world's biggest telescope, the 200-inch telescope on Palomar Mountain.

From the studies which astronomers have carried on during the past 300 years, we know the moon has a diameter of 2,163 miles. Our earth, as you know, has a diameter of 7,920 miles.

Some of the maria are very large and nearly circular in shape. Mare Imbrium is about 700 miles in diameter. Mare Serenitatis is 430 miles in diameter.

There are ten great mountain ranges on the moon. These have been named after mountain ranges on earth. So we speak of the Lunar Alps, the Lunar Apennines and so on. These mountain ranges are extremely rugged and have many tall peaks.

The largest range is the Lunar Apennines which runs along one side of the Mare Imbrium in a great curve 640 miles long. It contains more than 3,000 tall peaks, some of them as much as 18,000 feet high.

The scene which greets our eyes as our space ship swings around the moon is very different from any we have ever seen on earth.

The most startling features are the craters. These are

everywhere. They look like extinct volcanoes, but they are not all alike and they range in size from very small ones, just barely visible at our altitude of 200 miles, to some more than 100 miles in diameter.

The lunar map-makers named the craters for the most part after the astronomers of their day. We find craters named Copernicus, Tycho, Kepler, and so on. The largest crater on the moon is named Clavius. It is 146 miles in diameter. There are about 32,000 craters on the face of the moon which we see from the earth.

Many of the craters are flat plains walled in by a ring of mountains. In general, the floor of a crater is lower than the nearby lunar surface, but some of the craters appear to be partially filled with what is either lava or dust.

Other craters have saucer-shaped interiors while yet others have mountain peaks rising from their center.

The rougher areas of the moon's surface are covered with a confused hodgepodge of craters. There are big ones and little ones. There are craters within craters and craters that have broken through the walls of other craters.

We see other strange and interesting features of the moon's surface from our space ship. There are long, straight cliffs, some of them more than fifty miles long.

They are thought to have resulted from the settling of large blocks of the moon's surface.

We also see deep cracks in the moon's surface. These are known as rills and sometimes extend for 90 or 100 miles.

A very strange feature are the light-colored streaks extending in all directions from some of the larger craters. Astronomers call them rays. They run over mountains and valleys in almost straight lines.

After circling the moon a number of times, our pilot decides to spiral downward and finally to land our ship gently on the Mare Imbrium near the base of the Lunar Apennines. We cannot leave our ship until we have donned our space suits.

However beautiful the moon may appear from earth, it is a dangerous and inhospitable place to visit. There is neither air nor water on the moon. The towering mountains are bare rock. There are no rushing mountain streams, no forests of pine and spruce, no carpets of grass.

The direct rays of the sun beat down upon the lunar surface. There is no blanket of air to protect us from them.

Because the moon turns so slowly on its axis, making

one revolution in the same time that it goes once around the earth, any given spot on the moon has approximately two weeks of sunlight, followed by two weeks of darkness.

During the long lunar day, the temperature rises until it is the temperature of boiling water, 212 degrees Fahrenheit. During the long lunar night, the temperature falls until it is 243 degrees below zero.

It will be necessary, therefore, for our space suits to be air-conditioned if we are going to travel about the moon's surface.

We find that the surface of the moon is covered with a thick layer of pulverized rock and dust. This makes it extremely difficult for us to get about since the dust fills the ruts and cracks and tiny craters in the moon's surface. We must be extremely careful, for some of the cracks may be very deep and in places the dust may hide sharp ridges and spikes of rock.

However, the fact that the moon's force of gravity is so small is a help. It is only one-sixth of what the force of gravity is on earth. Consequently, we find that we can leap 25 feet into the air without any difficulty.

There is a constant rain of meteors upon the surface of the moon. Much of the layer of pulverized rock on the lunar surface is the result of this bombardment.

Two theories have been advanced to account for the craters on the moon. One is that they are volcanoes which formed in the early days of the moon. The other is that they are the result of the impact of meteors.

It is thought that in the early days of the solar system there may have been many more large meteors than there are now. These huge meteors, crashing into the surface of the moon, may have created the craters.

You may wonder why there are not craters of this sort on earth. There is one in Arizona, known as Meteor Crater.

At one time there may have been many more on the earth. But the changes brought about by wind and rain and rushing rivers and the other forces of erosion have long since worn them away.

On the moon, because there is no air or water, there are no forces of erosion. And so the craters are still there.

Astronomers would like to visit the moon so that they could settle many problems about the moon. These include the origin of the craters, the nature of the mysterious rays, the composition of the rocks that form the moon, and so on.

There is also the possibility that the moon may contain precious ores and valuable minerals. Perhaps someday, we shall operate mines on the moon and bring silver and gold and platinum back to earth, the gifts of the Man in the Moon.

15 The Atomic Space Ship

Once the courageous explorers of space have landed on the moon, their next goal will be the planet Mars. No member of the solar system has attracted as much attention as Mars.

At times it shines in the evening sky like a great red lantern. Then, astronomers in all parts of the world turn their telescopes upon the ruddy planet. It is then closest to the earth, and they have their best chance of solving its riddles.

Such a close approach of the earth and Mars takes place every two years and two months.

The earth, as you know, is 93 million miles from the sun and takes 365¼ days to make one revolution around it. Mars is 141 million miles from the sun and takes 687 days for one revolution.

The distance between the earth and Mars changes

from day to day, since both are going around the sun with different speeds. When they are on opposite sides of the sun, they are farthest apart.

They are closest together when they are on the same side of the sun and situated so that a line from the sun to Mars passes through the earth. This happens once every two years and two months.

Astronomers call this event an "opposition." Because the orbits of both planets are ellipses, the exact distance separating the two at opposition depends upon where opposition takes place.

The distance at opposition averages 48 million miles. But it can be as much as 62 million and as little as 36 million.

You can see from this that it will take longer to get to Mars than to the moon. The moon is only 240,000 miles away. But it may surprise you to learn that getting to Mars will not be very much harder than getting to the moon.

It may also surprise you to know that space navigators will not start for Mars when the planet is closest to the earth. It would require more fuel than a space ship can carry to go in a straight line from the earth to Mars.

The trick will be to put the space ship into a proper

orbit and then let it coast to Mars. You will recall from Chapter 8 that this was the plan for getting to the moon.

A number of rocket experts, including Dr. Wernher von Braun, have designed Martian space ships using liquid fuels, such as hydrazine and nitric acid.

Such a ship will be built, of course, at the space station and will take off from there. It will weigh 1700 tons. A considerable portion of this weight will be the propellants. The cabin will have room for six or eight persons.

Since the Martian space ship will be built at the space station, it will already be circling the earth with the same speed as the space station. The pilot will only have to fire the rocket motors long enough to increase this speed to 25,000 miles per hour, the speed required for escaping from the earth's gravitational pull.

Once the space ship has escaped from the earth's gravitational field, it will be moving in an orbit around the sun. For all practical purposes, it will be a tiny planet, going around the sun like the earth and Mars.

The trick now will be for the pilot to adjust the speed of the space ship so that its orbit will be an ellipse with its low point at the space station and its high point at the orbit of Mars.

The Martian space ship will now coast halfway around the sun to the orbit of Mars. The journey must be planned correctly so that the space ship will meet up with Mars. It will take the ship 260 days to get to Mars.

When the ship enters the gravitational field of Mars, the pilot will put it into an orbit which will keep it circling about Mars at an altitude of about 600 miles.

The space ship will not attempt to land on Mars. It will carry a small rocket ship equipped with wings for making a landing through the Martian atmosphere and for returning again to the space ship.

The space ship will have to wait for the right moment to start back. The whole trip from the earth to Mars and back will take two and a half years.

Many scientists think that atomic energy will prove more satisfactory than liquid fuels as the source of power for a Martian space ship. They believe that an atomic space ship will be lighter in construction and easier to navigate.

Such an atomic space ship has been designed by Dr. Ernst Stuhlinger, one of the experts of the U. S. Army's rocket center at Huntsville, Alabama.

The appearance of Dr. Stuhlinger's atomic space ship

will startle you. It doesn't look like a rocket. It doesn't look like an airplane. It doesn't look like any of the designs for space ships that you have ever seen.

It looks like a gigantic umbrella or Japanese parasol. But it is a parasol that is 250 feet in diameter, and it has a stick which is 250 feet long. The illustration will help you understand it.

This umbrella-like ship weighs 730 tons. The nuclear reactor is located at the bottom of the stick where you would find the handle of an ordinary umbrella.

Living quarters for the crew and passengers are in a circular cabin at the top of the umbrella. A heavy shield of lead, just above the nuclear reactor, protects the occupants of the cabin from its dangerous radiations.

The heat of the reactor is used to turn a liquid, silicon oil, into a vapor or steam. The steam goes up a pipe through the stick of the umbrella and is used to operate a steam turbine just below the umbrella top.

Attached to the turbine is an electric generator. The energy of the nuclear reactor is being used, therefore, to generate electricity.

The top of the umbrella is really a great hollow vessel. The steam from the turbine enters it. Here it cools very quickly, condenses into a liquid again, and flows back

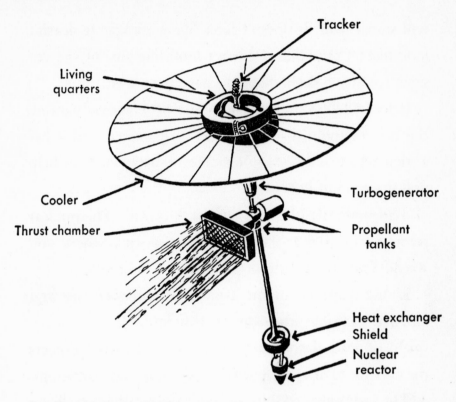

Tracker

Living
quarters

Cooler

Thrust chamber

Turbogenerator

Propellant
tanks

Heat exchanger
Shield

Nuclear
reactor

Dr. Stuhlinger's atomic space ship is like a gigantic parasol.

to the nuclear reactor to be turned into steam once more.

The rocket motor which drives the atomic space ship is mounted on the stick, halfway between the top of the umbrella and the handle. It differs from the motors which use ordinary propellants.

Rocket motors using liquid or solid fuels eject a train of heated gases. This motor ejects a stream of electrified particles.

The motor consists of two parts. There is a tank filled with some alkaline metal like cesium. This is heated just enough to cause the metal to vaporize. The vapor then enters a chamber where it comes into contact with a heated platinum grid.

This causes the cesium vapor to become ionized or electrified. The current produced by the turbo-generator is now used to speed up these electrified atoms or ions and to eject them from the nozzle at the back of the rocket motor.

In this way, the atomic space ship is propelled through space by a train of electrified particles.

Navigating the atomic space ship will differ in some ways from the handling of a ship using liquid fuels. The motor of the atomic ship will be kept in operation during almost all of the flight. This will be possible because of the nature of the power system.

The atomic ship will not gain speed as rapidly as the conventional type. For this reason the journey to Mars will be longer.

Leaving the space station, the atomic ship will spiral around the earth, gradually gaining speed since its motor will be in operation all the time.

Two hours after its take-off, the atomic space ship

will be only 20 miles from the space station. But at the end of 100 days of steady spiraling, it will be halfway to the moon.

A few days later, its speed will be sufficient for it to escape from the earth's gravitational field. It will then head for the planet Mars.

When the ship approaches Mars, the pilot will change its course into an orbit around the planet. No attempt will be made to land on Mars with the atomic space ship.

Instead, the atomic ship will carry a small, conventional rocket ship with wings which will be used for descending to the surface of the planet and returning to it.

Rocket experts agree that it would be unwise for a single space ship of any type to set out for Mars. At least two ships, or even five or six, would start out together. In this way, it would not be so dangerous if something went wrong with one of the ships.

If two ships were moving close to each other, it would be possible for passengers in space suits to transfer from one to the other.

A fleet of ships would also make possible a larger party of scientists and engineers for the exploration of the planet.

16 The Riddle of Mars

Is there life on Mars? That is the big question that astronomers have debated for more than a century. Opinions have changed with each new discovery about the planet.

At the close of the last century, many astronomers were certain that Mars was inhabited by intelligent beings. Today most astronomers do not believe so.

At each close approach of Mars, many astronomers in all parts of the world give the largest portion of their time to the study of the ruddy planet. These close approaches, you will recall, take place every two years and two months.

Then Mars glows in the sky like a flaming red lamp, and many people who hardly ever look at the stars are startled and surprised by it.

The astronomers have learned a great deal about the planet by studying it with their telescopes and with various other pieces of apparatus attached to their telescopes.

But they are now looking forward eagerly to the day when the first space ship will land on Mars. They believe that many of the questions concerning the planet can only be settled by an actual visit.

Let us see what astronomers have been able to find out so far about Mars with their telescopes and other instruments. Mars, you will recall, is approximately 141 million miles from the sun.

The planet has a diameter of 4,215 miles, a little more than half the diameter of the earth. The planet turns on its axis in a period of 24 hours, 37 minutes and 22 seconds. It takes 687 days to go once around the sun.

This means that the day on Mars is only a little longer than a day on earth, but a Martian year is almost equal to two of ours. Consequently each of the four seasons is almost twice as long on Mars as on the earth.

Mars is tipped on its axis at an angle that is approximately the same as the tilt of the earth's axis. This is approximately 23 1/2 degrees.

Like the earth, Mars is slightly flattened at the poles. Because of its smaller size, the force of gravity on Mars is only about 38 per cent of what it is on the earth.

Even a very small telescope reveals that Mars is an object of surprising beauty. The planet as a whole has a reddish or somewhat orange color when seen in the telescope.

However, an irregular belt running across the middle of the planet is darker in color, having bluish-gray, bluish-green, and greenish shades.

The white polar caps are seen easily with even a very small telescope.

Astronomers have been particularly interested in studying the seasonal changes in Mars. These changes have been responsible in considerable part for the belief that there may be life on Mars.

The reddish areas show very little change with the Martian seasons. Most astronomers are inclined to think that they are great rocky or sandy deserts.

Changes in the dark areas are very marked, and they go through regular cycles in the course of the Martian year. They seem to be connected with changes in the polar caps.

With the approach of spring in the northern hemisphere of Mars, the northern polar cap begins to shrink and grow smaller. It may disappear entirely. At the same time, the green areas in the northern hemisphere grow darker in color and become more conspicuous.

The change in color first takes place near the North Pole. But it gradually spreads down to the equator. These areas remain green throughout the summer. But in the autumn they begin to turn brown. At the same time, the polar cap begins to grow larger again.

The same changes take place in the southern hemisphere. However, just as on earth, it is winter in the southern hemisphere when it is summer in the northern hemisphere.

Watching these changes, it is easy to imagine that there is dense vegetation on Mars and that the planet must be inhabited. This was the popular opinion at the close of the nineteenth century.

In addition to the division of the planet's surface into the reddish areas and the greenish areas, there also appears to be a wealth of other markings on the planet's surface. These are difficult to see with even the best telescopes. As a result there has been a great deal of argument about them.

In the year 1877, the Italian astronomer, G. V. Schiaparelli, announced that he had discovered a network of fine, straight lines on the surface of Mars. He called these "canali," which is the Italian word for "channels." However, the word was translated as "canals."

This caused great excitement and made it more certain than ever in the minds of many people that the planet must be inhabited.

The American astronomer, Percival Lowell, believed that the whole surface of the planet was covered with a complex network of such canals. These canals crossed each other and frequently four or more met at a point, forming what he called an oasis.

This led to the conclusion that the canals were artificial and had been dug by the inhabitants of Mars. It was easy to imagine that their purpose was to irrigate the Martian fields and farms with the water of the melting polar caps.

However, many astronomers insisted that they could see nothing remotely resembling straight lines on the surface of Mars but only a confused hodgepodge of marks. This is still the case today.

Most astronomers today doubt that there is a system of canals on Mars, but they are equally certain that there are surface features of some kind.

It has been suggested that these markings might represent old river beds or the beds of lakes that have long since dried up. Another suggestion is that they are cracks in the surface of Mars.

Recent studies incline most astronomers to the view that in all probability there is no intelligent life on Mars, at best only simple plant life.

Studies with spectroscopes and other equipment show that Mars has very little atmosphere. It is far thinner than that of the earth and probably only about 60 miles high.

The most recent studies show that the atmosphere of Mars contains less than five per cent of the amount of water vapor present in the atmosphere of the earth.

There is even less oxygen in the Martian atmosphere. It is less than one-tenth of one per cent of the amount present in our atmosphere.

The atmosphere of Mars, however, is thought to contain about twice as much carbon dioxide as the atmosphere of the earth.

Two kinds of clouds are observed on Mars. There are white clouds at the top of the atmosphere which are thought to be thin mist or crystals of ice.

Yellow clouds occur at low levels. These are thought to be dust clouds, rising from the red deserts.

Temperature measurements of Mars have been made by attaching an electrical thermometer known as the thermocouple to a telescope.

\These studies indicate that the temperature in the green areas at noon in summertime may be as high as 86 degrees Fahrenheit. However, the temperature falls very rapidly at night because the air on Mars is so thin. It falls to 9 degrees at sunset and to 150 degrees below zero at midnight. This is much too cold for life as we know it.

The great speed with which the polar caps form in winter and melt in summer has convinced astronomers that they are not ice fields like our own Arctic regions but merely thin layers of snow, perhaps only two or three inches deep.

Using special equipment, Dr. Gerald Kuiper, director of the Yerkes and McDonald Observatories, has studied the reflection of sunlight from the green areas of Mars. He has also compared it with the reflection from mountainsides covered with green foliage here on earth.

From these studies, he has concluded that the vegetation on Mars consists only of such lowly forms as mosses and lichens.

Many astronomers feel that Mars is a dying world

which has lost most of its oxygen and water vapor and so is slowly drying up.

The big question is whether intelligent beings ever lived on the planet and, if so, whether or not they have survived. It has been suggested that the inhabitants of Mars may live in underground cities.

These are questions which must wait until a space ship lands on the red planet.

17 The Solar System

Venus will be the second planet which space explorers will try to reach. Getting to Venus will be no harder than reaching Mars.

Venus and Mars are the planets nearest us. Mars is on one side of us, Venus on the other.

Later, scientists, and particularly astronomers, will want to visit the other planets. There are nine in the sun's family of planets.

Mercury is closest to the sun. Then comes Venus. Our own earth is next. It is followed by Mars, Jupiter, Saturn, Uranus, Neptune and Pluto. Between Mars and Jupiter are more than a thousand tiny planets known as the asteroids. They are thought to be the remnants of a planet that exploded or fell apart in some way.

Astronomers divide the planets into the terrestrial planets and the major planets. The terrestrial planets are the first four and get their name from the fact that they resemble the earth in many ways. The next four are all very much larger than the earth, and so they are called the major planets.

This leaves Pluto, which seems to be in a class by itself. However, it is about the size of the earth.

Let us look at these planets, starting with Mercury. We shall see that there is little possibility of life on any of them with the exception of Mars.

Many people go through life without ever seeing the planet Mercury. This is because the planet is never very far from the sun and so is ordinarily lost in the bright glare of sunlight.

At times it can be seen very low in the western sky at twilight. At other times it is low in the eastern sky just before sunrise.

Mercury is the smallest of all the planets. It is only a little larger than our moon. It has a diameter of 3,100 miles and is approximately 40 million miles from the sun.

The little planet takes 88 days to go once around the sun. It turns once upon its axis in the same time. As a result, it always keeps the same face turned toward the sun just as our moon always keeps the same face turned toward the earth.

Because of this, Mercury is at once the hottest and the coldest of all the planets. Measurements show that the sunlit face of Mercury has a temperature of 770 degrees Fahrenheit, a temperature that is sufficient to melt tin and lead.

The other side of Mercury has a temperature of about 400 degrees below zero.

The surface of the planet appears to be a rocky desert. There is no atmosphere. Under the circumstances, astronomers are certain that life does not exist on Mercury.

Venus is the brightest and most beautiful of all the planets. When it appears in the western sky at sunset, it is called the "evening star." When it shines in the eastern sky before sunrise, it is the "morning star."

It is about the same size as the earth, having a diameter of 7,700 miles. It is about 67 million miles from the sun and takes 225 of our days to go once around the sun.

Venus approaches closer to the earth than any of the other planets. At its closest, it is only 26 million miles away.

You might think, therefore, that we would know more about Venus than we do about Mars. But actually, Venus is an even greater mystery.

This is because Venus is covered with a dense layer

of clouds so thick that we cannot see through it. We never see the surface of the planet. We cannot even be sure how long it takes the planet to turn on its axis. Astronomers think it turns once every two or three weeks.

Astronomers have studied the portion of the atmosphere of Venus above the cloud layer. It does not seem to have any oxygen or water vapor, but it has an immense amount of carbon dioxide.

It is hard to explain what the clouds are made of since there seems to be no water vapor in the atmosphere of Venus. One theory is that the ultraviolet light of the sun has caused the water vapor on Venus to combine with the carbon dioxide to form formaldehyde. This substance is used on earth to make plastics. If the theory is right, then the clouds on Venus are made of plastic.

What about the temperature on the surface of Venus? Most astronomers think that it must be hotter than boiling water, a temperature too high for life as we know it.

The third planet in order from the sun is our own earth. Mars is fourth. Then come the giant planets.

Jupiter is the big brother of the solar system. It is the largest of the sun's family of planets, having a diameter of 86,720 miles.

The telescope reveals Jupiter as an object of great

beauty. It looks like a golden disk crossed by light and dark bands or belts.

The equatorial belt is bright, ranging in color from pale yellow to dull red. Above and below are darker belts, ranging from reddish-brown to bluish-grey. Other belts cover the planet's surface to the north and south.

These belts vary in appearance from year to year. Other features appear on the planet from time to time. In 1878 a great red spot appeared. This has gradually faded but can still be seen faintly with a powerful telescope.

Astronomers are certain that Jupiter is very different from our earth and the other terrestrial planets.

They believe that Jupiter consists of a rocky core about 40,000 miles in diameter. This is covered by a layer of ice about 20,000 miles thick. The temperature of this ice is about 200 degrees below zero, Fahrenheit.

Above the ice there is an atmosphere of hydrogen gas in which float thick clouds of ammonia and methane. It is the outer surface of these clouds which we see in the telescope.

Astronomers believe that conditions on Saturn, Uranus and Neptune are like those on Jupiter.

Little Pluto is the outermost planet of the solar system. It is so very far away that we know very little about it, but astronomers are certain that it is far too cold for life as we know it.

18 Into the Milky Way

On a clear moonless night, the stars seem countless. Actually they are not. From any given place on the earth's surface, you can count about 2,000 stars with the unaided eye.

But the number of stars increases if you scan the heavens with prism binoculars or a small telescope. To the unaided eye, the Milky Way looks like a silvery streak across the sky. Even a small telescope reveals that the Milky Way consists of thousands upon thousands of stars.

The larger the telescope we turn upon the heavens, the more stars we see. There are millions of stars within the range of the giant telescopes such as the 100-inch telescope on Mt. Wilson and the 200-inch telescope on Palomar Mountain.

We know now that every star is a gigantic, glowing

globe of heated gases like our own sun. Every star is a sun. Or to put it the other way around, our sun is the particular star around which our earth revolves.

Our sun is just one of a hundred billion stars in our galaxy. These hundred billion stars are scattered in space in a formation like a very thin pocket watch.

The reason you see so many stars in the narrow band of the Milky Way is because you are looking along the hands of the watch. You are looking into the depths of the galaxy. When you look at other parts of the sky, you are looking out through the face or the back of the watch.

What are the chances of our space ships sailing out beyond the solar system some day, past Jupiter and the other major planets, past little Pluto, past the comets at the very edge of the sun's domain?

To answer this question we must know something about the distances in the galaxy.

You will recall that it is 240,000 miles from the earth to the moon. It is 93 million miles from the earth to the sun. It is more than three and a half billion miles to Pluto.

See how the scale of distances increases. First we used thousands of miles, then millions, then billions.

To measure the distances to the stars, we must use trillions of miles. The nearest star is 25 trillion miles away.

Astronomers use a yardstick which they call the light-year. This is the distance which a beam of light travels in a year. The speed of light is 186,000 miles a second. In a year, light travels six trillion miles.

The nearest star is approximately four and a third light-years away. Other stars are ten light-years away; still others 100 light-years.

More than half the stars visible to the unaided eye are more than 400 light-years away. The most distant stars in the Milky Way are about 100,000 light-years away.

By now, you see the problem involved in journeying beyond the solar system. If we traveled with the speed of light, 186,000 miles a second, it would still take us four and a third years to reach the nearest star. This is a star in the southern hemisphere known as Alpha Centauri.

Perhaps you are familiar with some of the bright stars. Sirius, the Dog Star, brightest of all the stars, is approximately eight and a half light-years away. It would take eight and a half years for a space ship traveling with the speed of light to get there.

But nothing can travel as fast as light. This is one of the strange facts about the universe first pointed out by Dr. Albert Einstein in his theory of relativity. Someday it may be possible to build space ships that will travel almost as fast as light, perhaps with even 99.99 per cent of the speed of light.

However, to attain such speeds will take tremendous amounts of power. At the present time we do not know how to do it.

A strange thing would happen if we could travel with speeds approaching the speed of light. This is also something which Einstein pointed out in his theory of relativity.

Einstein showed that our measurements of time depend upon the speed with which we are moving. The faster you move, the more slowly your clock goes. On earth this is not important because the greatest possible speed makes a difference in the rate of the clock that is still too small to measure.

But if you left the earth in a space ship with a speed approaching that of light, it would make a very great difference. According to the clocks on earth, you might be gone a hundred years. But according to the space-ship clock, you would have been away only an hour.

The big question is what would happen to you on the journey. Would you grow one hour older or would you grow 100 years older?

Scientists think that you would be only an hour older. The reason for this is that every atom in your body is a clock. The electrons are going around the nucleus just as the hands of the clock go around the dial.

All the atoms in your body would slow down just as the clock on the wall did. All the functions of your body would slow down in the same way. You would not be aware of the flight of time on earth. You would only have time to eat your dinner in the space ship while a whole century rolled by on earth.

It would, of course, be impossible for a space ship to get very close to a star because of the temperature. Many stars are far hotter than our own sun.

It may be, however, that many of the stars have families of planets like our own sun. Let us suppose that only one out of every million stars has a family of planets. This would still mean about 100,000 such families.

Astronomers feel that some of these planets must be inhabited by intelligent beings.

Our galaxy is only a small part of the universe. Far

out in space there are many other galaxies or collections of stars like our own. Astronomers call them the exterior galaxies or the spiral nebulae.

But the nearest one is so far away that its light takes more than a million years to reach us. It seems, therefore, that even with the best of space ships, men will be able to explore only a small corner of the universe.

However, it is too early to try to predict the future of space travel. The first airplane, built by the Wright brothers in 1903, stayed in the air less than a minute on its first flight. Goddard's first liquid-fuel rocket stayed up for two and a half seconds.

The first artificial satellites were launched in 1957. The Age of Space Travel has only begun.

Index

Aerobee rocket, 30, 60, 68, 91
Alpha Centauri, 156
Alps, Lunar, 126
Anderson, O. A., 8
Apennines, Lunar, 126, 128
Apogee, 86
  of Explorer I, 39
  of Explorer III, 40
  of lunar space ship, in orbit around earth, 117
  of Moon Messenger, 87
  of Sputnik I, 77
  of Sputnik II, 80
  of Vanguard I, 51
Army Ballistic Missile Agency, 32
Atmosphere, cosmic rays in, 7, 8, 12
  density of, 7, 8
  electrified layers of, 7, 12
  exploration of, 7-8
  at height of 250 miles, 3
  humidity of, 7
  information to be gained about, 7, 52
  jet streams in, 11
  layers of, 7, 8, 9, 10, 11, 12, 13
  and magnetic field of earth, 8
  meteors in, 6, 7, 8, 12, 13
  pressure of, 7
  temperatures of, 6, 7, 8, 10, 11, 12, 13
  ultraviolet rays in, 7, 8, 11, 12
  upper, 6, 7, 9, 10, 11, 12, 13
  winds in, 7, 11
Atomic energy, 2, 135
Atomic space ship, 2, 135-39
Aurora Borealis (Northern Lights), 6, 7, 12

Balloons, atmosphere explored by, 6, 7, 57

Barr cart, 15, 16
Bell X-1, 103
Black, Samuel, 101
Brennschluss (burn-out), 48

California Institute of Technology, 36
Cape Canaveral, 4, 34, 38, 40, 46, 48, 51
Centrifuge, 92
Cesium, 137, 138
Chinese, rockets made by, 23-24
Clavius Crater, on moon, 127
Cosmic rays, 7, 8, 12, 16, 39, 52, 56, 79, 97, 108
Crane, gantry, 15, 16, 36, 58, 59, 122

Dimethyl hydrazine, 44
Dog(s), in Russian rockets, 91
  in Sputnik II, 79, 80, 91-92
Dornberger, Walter, 28

Earth, craters on, 130
  diameter of, 126
  distance from sun, 132, 155
  exact shape determined through satellites, 73, 74
  gravitational field of, 80, 81
  magnetic field of, 8
  maps corrected through satellites, 73-74
  photographed from air, 8
  revolution around sun, 132
  seen from space station, 112-13
Ehricke, Krafft A., 84
Einstein, Albert, 157
Escape velocity, 87
Exosphere, 10, 13
Experimental space cabin, 69

Explorer I, 4, 34, 35, 39-40, 61
Explorer II, 40
Explorer III, 40, 66

Farrell, Donald G., 69
Fireworks, 23, 24, 26
Free fall, 94

Galileo, 124, 125
Gamow, George, 84
Gantry crane, 15, 16, 36, 58, 59, 122
Geiger counter, 39, 56, 108
Goddard, Robert Hutchins, 26, 27, 83, 159
Goodyear Aircraft Corporation, 101
Gravity, on Mars, 142
  on moon, 121, 129
  satellites kept in orbit by, 80, 81
  and take-off, withstanding force of, 92-93
  zero, 94, 95
Gyroscopes, in rockets, 16, 36, 45-46

Haber, Fritz and Heinz, 95
Hagen, John P., 41
Helium, 29, 42, 44
Huntsville, Ala., 32, 135
Hydyne, 34
Hydrogen bomb, and Moon Messenger, 84
Hydrogen peroxide, 30, 41

Intercontinental ballistic missiles, 83
International Geophysical Year, 32-33, 76
Ionosphere, 9, 10, 12

Jet streams, 11
Jupiter, 148, 151, 152, 155
Jupiter-C rocket, 4, 34, 35, 36, 37, 39, 40, 61, 62, 63, 64, 65

Kincheloe, Ivan, 8, 103, 104, 105
Knight, Richard E., 101
Kuiper, Gerald, 146

Light, speed of, 156, 157
Light-year, defined, 156
Liquid oxygen, 17
Lowell, Percival, 144
Lunar space ship, 115–23
  built at space station, 115, 116
  cabin of, 116
  landing on moon, 118, 120
  in orbit around earth, 116–17
  in orbit around moon, 117, 118
  return to earth, 117
  Romick's plan for, 120–22
  speed of, 116

Magnesium, 53
Magnetic field of earth, 8
Mare Imbrium, 125, 126, 128
Mare Serenitatis, 125, 126
Mare Tranquilitatis, 125
Mars, 2, 108, 148, 149, 151
  atmosphere of, 145
  "canals" of, 144
  clouds on, 145
  dark areas of, 142
  diameter of, 141
  distance from earth, 132–33
  distance from sun, 132, 141
  gravity on, 142
  greenish areas of, 143, 146
  journey to, 133–35, 138–39
  life on, 140, 142, 143, 145, 146, 147
  markings on surface of, 144–45
  polar caps of, 142, 143, 146
  reddish areas of, 140, 142, 143
  revolution around sun, 132, 141
  rotation on axis, 141
  seasons on, 141, 142, 143
  temperatures on, 146
  tipped on axis, 141
Massachusetts Institute of Technology, 73
Mercury, 148, 149, 150
Meteor Crater, on earth, 130
Meteor Junior rocket, 72, 101–03, 106, 110, 111, 119, 120
Meteors, 6, 7, 8, 12, 13, 39, 40, 52, 55, 107
  rain upon moon, 129–30
Mice, in Aerobee rocket, 91
Milky Way, 154–59
Minitrack radio, 53, 54, 55
Minitrack receiving stations, 56, 76
Missiles, intercontinental ballistic, 83
Monkeys, in Aerobee rocket, 91
Moon, air lacking on, 128
  craters of, 71, 124, 125, 126–27, 128, 129, 130
  day on, length of, 129
  diameter of, 126
  distance from earth, 2, 87, 116, 133, 155,
  dust on surface of, 129
  exploration of, 124–31
  fall toward earth, 82
  as first goal of space travel, 1–2, 5, 115ff.
  gravity on, 121, 129
  journey to, 122–24
  maps of, 125
  maria of, 125, 126
  meteor rain on, 129–30
  minerals on, 131
  and Moon Messenger, 84–89
  mountain ranges of, 124, 125, 126
  night on, length of, 129
  other side seen by Moon Messenger, 5, 88
  photographs of, 125
  probable date of first journey to, 2
  rays extending from craters of, 128, 130
  rills of, 128
  rockets for circling, 84, 87, 88
  samples of, brought back by Moon Messenger, 89
  temperatures on, 129
  water lacking on, 128
  See also Lunar space ship
Moon Messenger, 84–89, 99, 116, 117
  escape velocity of, 87
  instruments in, 88, 89
  moon circled by, 84, 87, 88
  return to earth, 88, 89
Moonwatch Operation, 73, 76
Motion-picture camera, in Moon Messenger, 89
Motion sickness, 96
Motor, of atomic space ship, 137–38
  of Viking rocket, 42–43
Mt. Wilson, telescope at, 125, 126, 154
"Mouse," 31, 32

Naval Research Laboratory, 32, 41, 70
Nebulae, spiral, 159
Neptune, 148, 152
Newton, Isaac, 25, 80
Nitric acid, 44
Nitrogen, 29
Northern Lights, 6, 7, 12

Operation Moonwatch, 73, 76
Orbiter, Project, 32, 33
Oxygen, liquid, 17
Ozonosphere, 9, 10, 11

Palomar Mountain, telescope at, 125, 126, 154
Passenger-carrying rockets, 98–105
  constructed at space station, 98, 99, 108, 115, 116
  giant, 99–100, 106
  Meteor Junior, 72, 101–03, 106
Peenemünde, 27

Perigee, 86
  of Explorer I, 39
  of Explorer III, 40
  of lunar space ship in
    orbit around earth,
    116
  of Moon Messenger, 87
  of Sputnik I, 77
  of Sputnik II, 80
  of Vanguard I, 51
Photo-electric cell, in sat-
    ellite, 56
Pitch, of rocket, 43, 44
Pluto, 148, 149, 153, 155
Potassium permanganate,
    30
Project Orbiter, 32, 33
Project Vanguard, 33, 41–
    51

Radar, for tracking sat-
    ellite, 67, 73
Radio ceiling, 12
Radio cut-off mechanism,
    17
Radio stations, on Pacific
    islands, 74
Radio transmitter, 32, 37
  installed in Viking
    rocket, 17
  in satellite, 40, 53, 79
Radio waves, 7, 12
Randolph Air Force Base,
    93, 95, 96
Redstone rocket, 32, 34,
    35
Relativity, theory of, 157
Retro rockets, 50
Rocket(s), Aerobee, 30,
    60, 68, 91
  animals sent in, 90–92
  atmosphere explored
    by, 8
  for circling moon, 84,
    87, 88
  early, 23–25, 26
  electronic controls in,
    16, 37, 44, 46, 48
  in elliptical orbits, 86
  flight explained by third
    law of motion, 25–26,
    80
  four-stage, 4, 34, 35, 36,
    37, 38, 120–22
  Goddard's, 27, 159
  gyroscopes in, 16, 36,
    45–46

Jupiter-C, 4, 34, 35, 36,
    37, 39, 40, 61, 62, 63,
    64, 65
  liquid-fuel, 27, 29–30,
    34, 41, 44, 159
  Meteor Junior, 72, 101–
    03, 106, 110, 111, 119,
    120
  moon as goal of, 1–2, 5,
    83–89
  passenger-carrying, see
    Passenger-carrying
    rockets
  pitch of, 43, 44
  Redstone, 32, 34, 35
  retro, 50
  roll of, 43, 44
  single-stage, 14–22, 30,
    99
  solid-fuel, 28, 32, 36
  take-off by, force en-
    countered in, 93
  with television camera,
    4
  three-stage, 33, 41ff., 77,
    99, 100, 101–02, 106
  tracking course of, 21,
    38, 47
  with transmitter, 5
  transport, 108
  two-stage, 2
  Vanguard, see Van-
    guard rocket
  Viking, see Viking
    rocket
  V-2, 2, 3, 28, 29, 30, 32
  WAC Corporal, 2, 3, 9,
    57
  weightlessness in, 94, 95
  yaw of, 43, 44
  See also Moon Messen-
    ger; Space ship
Rocket plane, Bell X-1,
    103
  X-15, 9, 103–05
Roll, of rocket, 43, 44
Romick, Darrell C., 101,
    110, 120

Satellite(s), artificial, at-
    mosphere explored
    by, 8, 52
  first American (Explor-
    er I), 4, 34, 35, 39, 61,
    65
  instruments in, 39–40,
    52–56, 79

motion explained by
    Newton's laws, 80–81
  in orbit, 39, 40, 56
  Russian, 4, 33, 75–82
  testing of, 70
  unmanned, 31ff.
  Vanguard, see Van-
    guard satellite(s)
Saturn, 148, 152
Schiaparelli, G. V., 143–44
Singer, S. Fred, 31, 32
Sirius, 156
Skyhook balloon, 8, 57
Smithsonian Astrophysi-
    cal Observatory, 76
Space medicine, 90–97
  and animals on rocket
    flights, 90–92
  cosmic rays as problem
    for, 97
  design of space ships
    studied by, 96
  experiments with vol-
    unteers, 90, 92–93, 95–
    96
  take-off effects studied
    by, 92–93
  and temperatures en-
    dured by human be-
    ings, 97
  and weightlessness, 95,
    96
Space ship, atomic, 2, 135–
    39
  constructed at space sta-
    tion, 98, 99, 108, 115,
    116, 134
  lunar, see Lunar space
    ship
  Martian, 134, 138
  maximum speed of, 157
  moon as first goal of, 1–
    2, 5, 115ff.
  and time in relation to
    speed, 157–58
  von Braun's design of,
    134–35
  See also Moon Messen-
    ger; Rocket(s)
Space station, 98, 99, 100,
    106–14, 138
  earth seen from, 112–13
  instruments at, 108
  Romick's plan for, 110–
    12
  space ship built at, 98,
    99, 108, 115, 116, 134

stars seen from, 108, 112
sun seen from, 112
sunlight effects on, 114
von Braun's plan for, 107–09
wheel-shaped, 108–09
Space suit, 106, 113, 129, 139
Space taxi, 114
Sputnik I, 4, 33, 75–79
Sputnik II, 4, 75, 79–80, 91
Stars, distance to, 156
number in Milky Way, 154, 155
seen from space station, 108, 112
temperature of, 158
Stevens, Albert W., 8
Stratosphere, 9, 10, 11
Stuhlinger, Ernst, 38, 135ff.
Sun, interior of rocket heated by, 97
light effects on space station, 114
seen from space station, 112
studied at space station, 108
ultraviolet rays of, 7, 8, 11, 12, 56, 151

Take-off, cabin heated by, 96–97
withstanding force of, 93
Tape recorder, in satellite, 54, 66
Telemetering system, 53–54
Telescope(s), Galileo's, 124
Mars seen through, 132, 141, 142, 143
at Mt. Wilson, 125, 126, 154
at Palomar Mountain, 125, 126, 154
red spot of Jupiter seen through, 152
at space station, 108
stars seen through, 154
thermocouple attached to, 146
for tracking orbit of satellite, 56, 73

Television camera, in moon rocket, 4–5, 88
Thermistor, 54
Transmitter, radio, see Radio transmitter
Transport rocket, 108
Troposphere, 9, 10, 11

Ultraviolet rays, 7, 8, 11, 12, 56, 79, 151
Uranus, 148

Van Pelt, J. M., 101
Vanguard, Project, 33, 41–51
Vanguard rocket, 34, 41ff.
altitudes reached by different stages of, 48, 49
burn-out in first stage of, 48
diameter of, 41
electronic controls in, 44, 46, 48
firing of, 46–47
first stage of, 41–43, 47, 48
gyroscope in, 45–46
on launching platform, 46, 59
length of, 41
satellite launched by, 50–51
second stage of, 44, 49–50
third stage of, 44, 50
velocities of different stages of, 48, 49, 50
weight of, 41
Vanguard satellite(s), 33
apogee of, 51
cosmic rays measured by, 56
diameter of, 51, 53
earth's shape determined through, 73, 74
electronic brain in, 52, 53
gold-plated exterior of, 53
instruments in, 52–56
launching of, 46–51
made of magnesium, 53
magnetic memory of, 52, 53, 54, 55
maps corrected through, 73

meteor detectors in, 55
perigee of, 51
radar for tracking of, 67
radio transmitter in, 52, 53, 54
telemetering system in, 53–54
thermistor in, 54
tracking orbit of, 56, 73
ultraviolet rays measured by, 56
weather information gained by, 56
weight of, 53
Venus, 2, 148, 150, 151
Viking rocket, 14
and blockhouse, 14, 18
cut-off mechanism in, 17
firing of, 18–21
as first stage of Vanguard, 41
and fueling crew, 17
height reached by, 30
on launching platform, 14, 15, 16, 18
length of, 30
motor of, 42–43
radio transmitter installed in, 17
recovery of scientific instruments in, 21–22
von Braun, Werner, 28, 32, 34, 100, 107, 109, 134
V-2 rocket, 2, 3, 28, 29, 30, 32

WAC Corporal, 2, 3, 9, 57
Weather information, from Vanguard satellite, 56
Weather prediction, 7
Weightlessness, 94, 95, 96, 122
eliminated by centrifugal force, 108, 110
White Sands Proving Ground, 14, 30, 91

X-15, 9, 103–05

Yaw, of rocket, 43, 44